VEGAN WEIGHT LOSS
MANIFESTO

AN 8-WEEK PLAN TO CHANGE YOUR MINDSET, LOSE WEIGHT AND THRIVE

ZUZANA FAJKUSOVA & NIKKI LEFLER
FOUNDERS OF ACTIVE VEGETARIAN

PAGE STREET
PUBLISHING CO.

PAGE STREET
PUBLISHING CO.

First published in 2017 by
Page Street Publishing Co.
27 Congress Street, Suite 105
Salem, MA 01970
www.pagestreetpublishing.com

Distributed by Macmillan, sales in Canada by The Canadian Manda Group.

21 20 19 18 17   1 2 3 4 5

ISBN-13: 978-1-62414-380-9
ISBN-10: 1-62414-380-6

Library of Congress Control Number: 201793162

Cover and book design by Page Street Publishing Co.
Photography by Darina Kopcok

Printed and bound in China

  As a member of 1% for the Planet, Page Street Publishing protects our planet by donating to nonprofits like The Trustees, which focuses on local land conservation. Learn more at onepercentfortheplanet.org.

WE DEDICATE THIS BOOK TO YOU, THE READER.
MAY YOU FIND HEALTH AND HAPPINESS.

CONTENTS

PART 3
LET'S GET COOKING 61

PART 4
MY VEGAN KITCHEN 181

INTRODUCTION

Dear reader,

Both Nikki and I would like to thank you for picking up our book—we are excited to start this journey with you.

It's amazing how making one decision can change everything. Over fifteen years ago, I, Zuzana, made the choice to stop consuming animal products and start taking care of my physical health. Little did I know that this single decision would alter and shape every aspect of my life.

Throughout the years, I have learned many valuable lessons. Some came from books and research; others from trial and error. But, the majority of them came from hands-on experience. My career as a personal trainer and lifestyle coach allowed me the opportunity to directly apply my experience and knowledge to test what works and what doesn't.

In 2006, I met Nikki and we bonded instantly. Our shared passion for healthful eating, fitness and plant-based living inspired us to create www.activevegetarian.com. This blog became our way of helping people to take control of their own health and fitness, as well as a guide on how to live well in this fast-paced and ever-changing world.

But enough about us. This is about YOU.

Within the pages of this book, you will discover many answers about what it takes to truly thrive. We have compiled all of our knowledge and experience into one system that contains everything you need to take control of your own health. We hope that you will find many truths and gain a clearer insight into the world of plant-based living and physical fitness and get inspired to succeed on your personal journey.

We wish you all the best and are here to serve you.

With love and gratitude,

Zuzana & Nikki

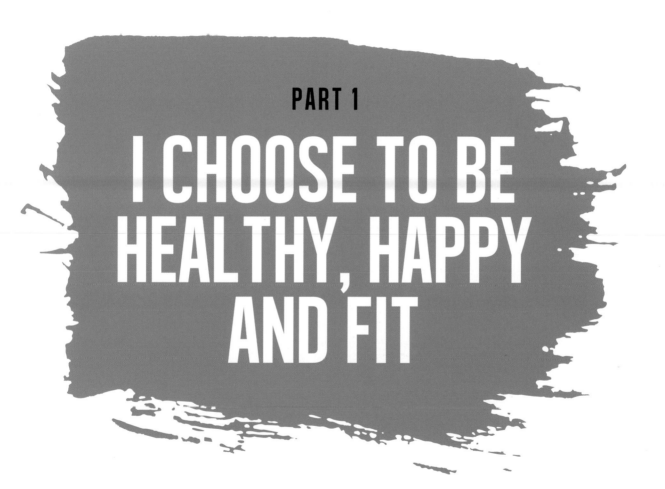

PART 1

I CHOOSE TO BE HEALTHY, HAPPY AND FIT

QUICK FIX OR A LIFESTYLE CHANGE?

"The starting point of all achievement is desire."

—*Napoleon Hill*

Before we dive into the nitty-gritty part of this plan, we want you to be honest and clear about what it is that you desire. Why did you pick up this book? What would you like to gain from the eight-week plan? What are you searching for?

Stop reading for a moment and answer the above questions.

Seriously, just do it. Now.

For some, the desire might be weight loss.

For some, it will be healing their body and preventing disease.

For others, it might be having more energy and a zest for life.

We have no idea what your dreams or desires are . . . but we do know that you have the power and ability to have the life you want. Every one of us has the potential to be happy, healthy and fit. Nikki and I want to help you realize that. Our desire is to help you elevate the state of your health and overall well-being.

There is a strong chance that you've picked up this book in hopes to lose weight, fast. Perhaps you feel that a vegan diet will get you there. And you are right. If you do follow the principles described in the following chapters, the excess weight will come off. We want you to know that with this eight-week plan, the potential is much greater than just weight loss.

Losing weight through dieting alone will not guarantee lasting success. It might temporarily change your outside appearance, but it won't leave a permanent change. You will be on a search for the next quick fix before you know it.

However, if you are sick of this roller coaster and have a strong desire to change and take charge of your own health, then Nikki and I will be here for you, guiding you and cheering you on. We are in this together.

Today is a fresh canvas: a new beginning and your beautiful opportunity to step into the life you dream of—to live.

WILL THIS WORK FOR ME?

There's something no one ever likes to admit about the path to health and getting in better shape: It takes time, determination and hard work.

As Nelson Mandela said, "It always seems impossible, until it's done." Fortunately, you don't have to do this alone. Nikki and I are here to help. Together we will embark on a journey to get you from where you are today to where you desire to be. As with any journey, it will have its challenges.

Some days the road will be sweet—enjoyable, surrounded by beauty—and other days it might lead you through rough terrain—full of challenges and obstacles standing in your way. The main focus is to keep on moving forward. Take it all in. It's all part of the process, the good, the bad and the ugly.

You picked up this book for a reason so let's make sure you follow through and fulfill that desire that sparked your interest! Trust that both Nikki and I are here to help you every step of the way.

We promise that if you follow the principles of this eight-week plan, you will succeed. You will feel lighter, younger and more energized. How can we be sure? Because we have seen many lives transformed. This approach to food and lifestyle has helped us and thousands of others heal from disease and restore their health. And we are confident it can help you, too.

Harvard Medical School reports that:

"The latest and best scientific evidence shows that a plant-based diet rich in vegetables, whole grains, healthy fats and healthy proteins lowers the risk of weight gain and chronic disease."[2]

Other plant-based diet benefits include the following:

- Anti-inflammatory properties
- Promoting weight loss
- Boosting energy levels
- Lowering risk of chronic diseases (cancer, heart disease, diabetes, high blood pressure)[3]
- Helping the environment

WHY VEGAN?

In 1944, the first Vegan Society was created in England and the name *vegan* was developed to differentiate vegans from vegetarians. They defined vegan like so:

"Vegans abstain from eating all meat, fish or fowl, as well as any other foods of animal origin such as butter, milk, yogurt, honey, eggs, gelatin or lard and any prepared foods containing these ingredients. Vegans typically avoid animal products in other domains too (e.g., leather products)."[4]

To be honest, we are not fans of labels. Nikki and I believe in the power of plants, we have compassion for all living beings and respect for the universe. Since adopting this way of being, our lives have changed on so many levels. For us, being vegan simply means strengthening our health, personal relationships and our relationship with our planet. We feel that everyone can benefit from this approach to life.

The recipes you will find in Part 3 (page 61) are free of meat, dairy, processed foods, gluten and eggs, and are considered vegan.

Our hope is to inspire many of you to incorporate healthy, quality food into your diet. Through personal experience, we know that structuring your meals around fruits, vegetables, nuts and seeds is a powerful way to live.

We don't care where you are in life or where have you been; Nikki and I are not here to judge you. Our mission is simple: We want to guide you to be strong, healthy and vibrant.

Don't wait! The time will never be "just right."

HOW TO GET THE MOST OUT OF THIS BOOK

You have in your hands a tool for changing your life, an eight-week plan for improving health and finding peace and happiness.

---

2   Harvard Health Publications. "Harvard researchers continue to support their healthy eating plate," last modified June 5, 2017, http://www.health.harvard.edu/harvard-researchers-launch-healthy-eating-plate.

3   Craig, Winston J, "Health effects of vegan diets," *The American Journal of Clinical Nutrition* (2009), doi: 10.3945/ajcn.2009.26736N.

4   The Vegan Society. "Ripened by human determination," last modified October 31, 2014, https://www.vegansociety.com/sites/default/files/uploads/Ripened%20by%20human%20determination.pdf.

This is not just a diet book. Our goal is to empower you with the knowledge and tools to thrive throughout a lifetime of enjoying optimal health. And that goes way beyond just the food you eat. Each of the eight weeks will be divided into three categories:

- Nutrition
- Fitness
- Lifestyle

Throughout the book, you will come across the following three icons:

ASSIGNMENTS

Every chapter we will be introducing three new assignments: one for Nutrition, one for Fitness and one for Lifestyle. When you see the above icon—this is your cue to get to work!

To some of you this might seem like a lot at once, but no need to panic! Just read on . . .

In the book *The Power of Less*[5], author Leo Babauta outlines his method of success, one that we also use with our clients. We found that *The Power of Less* is a sure way to form long-lasting habits: Focus on one habit, one change at a time, so this way you can channel all your energy on creating that change and making this habit a lifestyle.

With that said, in order to ensure your long-term success, we strongly suggest you move on to a new week only after you've fully completed all given assignments from the week you were currently on, even if it takes you longer than seven days!

We're not suggesting that you procrastinate and purposely put off those tasks, but we understand that life can get busy and you might have trouble staying consistent with the plan. Break it down, go slow and take action every day that will get you closer to your goal. Step by step, keep on moving forward!

Please don't overlook any part of this plan, no matter how uncomfortable or challenging it might feel. There is a method to our madness. If you decide to skip certain pieces, you will experience something similar to the domino effect. One seemingly small thing out of balance can lead to the entire system collapsing. If your desire is to get healthy and continue thriving, then it's crucial to complete all outlined assignments.

---

5   Babauta, Leo, *The Power of Less: The Fine Art of Limiting Yourself to the Essential. . . in Business and in Life* (New York: Hachette Books, 2009).

WEB SUPPORT

ACCOUNTABILITY

Nikki and I have learned over the years of working with clients that it's a lot easier to stay consistent when you've got a coach checking up on you. We would love to offer personal support to all of you but that's physically impossible. However, we are determined to help as many of you as possible and for that reason, we have created something super cool!

Whenever you see the Web Support icon, this notifies you that we have created additional support that is available at www.activevegetarian.com. What you can look forward to is additional material, including workout videos, weekly meal plans, extra recipes, motivational tips and more, all designed to support your eight-week journey.

With the purchase of this book, you will receive free eight-week access to the client-only area of our website. This is a very valuable tool and we encourage you to take full advantage of it.

We will also do our best to answer any of your questions that might surface along the way. Speaking of questions, here is the third and final icon you should take note of:

"WHAT IF?" QUESTIONS

This is an area where we address the most common questions and concerns that may arise. Okay, let's see how well you were paying attention . . .

YOUR FIRST ASSIGNMENT

GET ON BOARD

Go over to www.activevegetarian.com/veganweightlossmanifesto and create your free 8-week account using the code AV-VWM.

As soon as you register, you'll gain access to our personal support and all of the other extra tools to help you achieve positive results and reach your health and weight-loss goals.

Thank you for believing in us and what we do. Nikki and I are more committed than ever to helping you improve your health, get in the best shape possible and live a fulfilling, happy life. Let's do this together!

Now is your moment. Believe in your best. And let yourself shine!

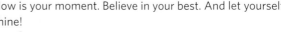

PART 2

I'M READY: LET'S DO THIS

WEEK 1

We are proud of you for making it this far into the book. You would be surprised how many people buy a book or sign up for a plan but never do anything with it. You are serious about making a lasting change, once and for all. High five! Now let's talk nutrition . . .

NUTRITION

"Let food be thy medicine and medicine be thy food."

—*Hippocrates*

Making dietary changes is far from easy. It's even more difficult to change your eating habits if you stay surrounded by all those "tempting" foods that have been a part of your everyday life for years.

And let's face it, if a certain food is in your house, car, purse or anywhere in your possession, either you or someone you care about will eventually eat it.

For that reason, your very first task will be to clean up your kitchen. Yes, that means all the junk (we mean all of it), restocked with nutritious, health-promoting foods.

You will need to go over all of the items in your pantry, refrigerator and freezer. We will give you clues on what to look for in order to determine how "safe" that particular item is. If it is safe, it stays; if the ingredients don't fit the provided criteria or you are unsure, then it goes. Simple as that.

STRUGGLING WITH THE IDEA OF THROWING AWAY FOOD?

Donate a box of perishable food to your local food bank. In the worst-case scenario, pack that box somewhere far away and keep it there for the duration of this plan. After eight weeks, you can decide what you want to do with it. But by then, we guarantee you will make the right decision.

PANTRY/REFRIGERATOR/FREEZER MAKEOVER

"If it came from a plant, eat it; if it was made in a plant, don't."

—*Michael Pollan,* Food Rules

Your task is to throw away all animal products (except honey); foods that contain chemicals such as preservatives, coloring or artificial flavors; and enriched foods and anything that will hinder your journey.

YOUR WEEK 1 NUTRITION ASSIGNMENT

OUT WITH THE JUNK AND IN WITH THE HEALTHY

STEP #1

Get a few large garbage bags and some cardboard boxes.

STEP #2

Go through your refrigerator, freezer and pantry—one by one—and throw away all of the following:

Animal Products

- Butter or cream
- Eggs
- Cheese
- Milk, cream, yogurt
- Meats, poultry, lamb or beef
- Processed meats such as hot dogs, bacon and deli meats
- Fish, shellfish, shrimp or lobster
- Gelatin

Junk Food

- Chips (of all kinds)
- Chocolates or candy
- Soda/pop and sweetened drinks, diet soda, sports drinks
- Alcohol, especially flavored/sweetened mixed drinks
- Instant foods like cake mixes, dried soups, mashed potatoes, flavored oatmeal packets
- Margarine and other processed fats
- Cooking oils (except high-quality organic coconut, hemp, flax or extra virgin olive oil)
- Frozen dinners/entrées
- Breads and bagels, unless they're made exclusively with whole sprouted grains
- Other baked goods

- Boxed breakfast cereals
- Crackers (even the whole-grain ones)
- Fruit, cereal and/or granola bars
- Peanut butter (any kind!)
- Fruit juice
- Takeout or restaurant leftovers
- Any other "snack-like" foods
- Condiments such as barbecue and other sweetened sauces
- Sweetened relishes, mustards and ketchup
- Salad dressings
- Sugars and sweeteners (except coconut sugar, maple syrup, honey, molasses and raw stevia)
- Bread crumbs, croutons and other dried bread products
- Nuts and seeds (keep raw ones, unless they smell rancid)

And trash any food that:[1]

- Contains ingredients that no ordinary human would keep in the pantry
- Arrived through the window of your car
- Contains high-fructose corn syrup
- Has more than five ingredients
- Has the word "light" or the terms "low-fat" or "non-fat" in its name
- You see advertised on television

What about meat substitutes?

I understand that Tofu Pups, Tofurky, veggie burgers, Fakin' Bacon and such could be appealing, especially to someone who is just starting to transition into a plant-based lifestyle, BUT . . . these products are far from healthy! In most cases what you get is highly processed, chemically altered, high in sodium and often genetically modified crap. So in other words, stay away.

---

1   Pollan, Michael, *Food Rules: An Eater's Manual* (London: Penguin Books, 2009).

STEP #3

Don't panic if your kitchen is totally bare. Take it as a new beginning; a clean slate.

WHAT IF I'M HAVING DOUBTS?

It's much easier to make a change and stick to a vegan lifestyle if you understand the science behind this approach. Why is eating vegan dramatically better for your health? Being clear about your whys is crucial for your success. If you are still contemplating and perhaps already questioning if throwing away all that junk food was one big mistake, you might need some help. I highly suggest watching one or more of the following documentaries:

- *Forks Over Knives*
- *Vegucated*
- *Earthlings*
- *Fat, Sick and Nearly Dead*
- *Simply Raw: Reversing Diabetes in 30 Days*

STEP #4

Plan your meals for the week.

Part three of this book is dedicated to variety of easy-to-make, tasty plant-based recipes. Go over to page 24 and put together a few days' worth of meal plans. Aim to plan four to seven days ahead, depending on how often you grocery shop.

WEEK 1 MEAL PLAN AVAILABLE AT WWW.ACTIVEVEGETARIAN.COM.

Here is a sample of what one day of meals should look like:

Our meal plans are based on five meals per day.

SAMPLE: MONDAY MEAL PLAN

For the full week meal plan, see Week #1 Meal Plan on page 24.

MONDAYmeal PLAN

MEAL #1 (Between 6am - 8am)	IMMUNE BOOSTER	PAGE 71
MEAL #2 (Between 8am - 10am)	ONE PIECE OF FRUIT (apple)	PAGE 19
MEAL #3 (Between 10am - 12pm)	CHICKPEA SALAD SANDWICH	PAGE 101
MEAL #4 (Between 12pm - 3pm)	ONE NO BAKE FIG CRUMB BAR	PAGE 145
MEAL #5 (Between 5pm - 8pm)	KITCHARI with BASIC GREEN SALAD	PAGE 91

STEP #5

Create a shopping list.

Your next task is to restock your kitchen with some healthy stuff. What goes on your shopping list will be based on the recipes you have selected for your four- to seven-day meal plan. Look at the ingredients for each of the selected recipes and create a shopping list of everything you will need to have on hand.

Warning! Your first grocery shopping trip may seem extreme, but just remember that this will restock your empty cupboards and give you the base you need. From here on out, it will mostly be picking up fresh goods or refilling random items.

See an example of what your shopping list might look like on page 19.

STEP #6

Go shopping.

STEP #7

Follow your meal plan as closely as you can.

STEP #8

For support, meal plans, detailed shopping lists and extra tips that will help you stay consistent, go to www.activevegetarian.com.

FITNESS

"An early-morning walk is a blessing for the whole day."

—Henry David Thoreau

YOUR BODY WAS MADE TO MOVE

Exercise is a key component of a healthy lifestyle. You cannot enjoy optimal health and well-being if you are sedentary. During the next eight weeks, you will learn to include healthy and enjoyable ways to increase movement in your day-to-day living.

SAMPLE SHOPPING LIST

VEGETABLES
raw/organic whenever possible

Arugula
Asparagus
Avocados
Beets/Beet Greens
Bell Peppers
Bok Choy
Broccoli
Brussels Sprouts
Cabbage
Carrots
Celery
Collards
Cucumbers
Eggplant
Garlic
Green Beans
Kale
Mushrooms
Olives
Onions
Parsnips
Peppers (all kinds)
Plantains
Pumpkin
Radish
Romaine Lettuce
Salad Greens, Mixed
Spinach
Squash
Sun–dried Tomatoes
Tomatoes
Turnips
Watercress
Wheat Grass
Yams

FRUITS
raw/organic whenever possible

Apple
Apricot

Banana
Blackberries
Blueberries
Cantaloupe
Cherries
Coconuts (young)
Cranberries
Dates
Figs
Grapefruit
Grapes
Goji Berries
Lemon
Lime
Nectarine
Orange
Papaya
Peaches
Pears
Pineapple
Plums
Pomegranate
Raspberries
Strawberries
Unsulfured Raisins
Watermelon

SEA VEGETABLES
Dulse
Kelp
Nori Sheets

NUTS & SEEDS
raw/unflavored

Almonds
Brazil Nuts
Chia Seeds
Flax Seeds
Hemp Seeds
Hazelnuts
Macadamia
Pecans
Pine Nuts
Pistachios

Pumpkin Seeds
Sesame Seeds
Walnuts
Nut Butters
Seed Butters
NO Peanuts

FATS & OILS
organic/unrefined

Coconut Oil
Cocoa Nibs
Olive Oil
Shredded Coconut
Sesame Oil
Tahini
Hemp Oil
NO Canola Oil

FLOURS
Chickpea
Spelt

GRAINS
Brown Rice
Buckwheat
Quinoa
Wild Rice
Whole Oats (GF)
Sprouted Grains:
- Breads
- Tortillas
- English Muffins

LEGUMES
raw & dried or cooked & canned

Adzuki Beans
Black Beans
Black-eyed Peas
Chickpeas
Edamame

Lentils (brown, red, green)
Peas (green, yellow)
Tempeh

BEVERAGES
Almond Milk
Coconut Milk
Coconut Water
Green Tea
Herbal Teas
Kombucha
Raw Vegetable Juices
Mineral Water
Spring Water (or filtered)

SPICES & HERBS
Basil
Black Pepper
Cardamon (ground)
Cayenne Pepper
Chili Pepper
Cilantro
Coriander Seeds
Cinnamon
Cloves
Cumin
Curry Powder
Dill
Fennel
Garlic
Ginger (fresh/dry)
Mint
Mustard Seeds
Nutmeg
Oregano
Paprika
Parsley
Rosemary
Sage
Tarragon
Thyme
Turmeric

SWEETENERS
in moderation

Raw Honey (not vegan)
Stevia
Maple Syrup
Molasses (blackstrap)

CONDIMENTS
Apple Cider Vinegar
Balsamic Vinegar
Celtic Sea Salt
Coconut Aminos
Cocoa (raw)
Extracts:
- Vanilla
- Almond
Hummus
Himalayan Salt
Miso Paste
Mustard (stone ground)
Nutritional Yeast

SUPPLEMENTS
Greens Powder
Omega Oil
Plant–Based Protein Powder

OCCASIONAL INDULGENCES
Wine
Dark Chocolate

This week you are going to start walking. Walking might not be the hottest new fitness trend out there, but don't let that fool you! There are many wonderful advantages to walking:

- Everyone knows how to do it.
- You can do it anywhere and anytime.
- No special equipment is required, just a good pair of shoes.
- If injured, you can still participate.
- It can help prevent potential injuries, or avoid them altogether.
- It doesn't matter how old you are.
- It can provide a complete workout, comparable to other forms of exercise.

At the beginning of my fitness career, I didn't give walking enough credit. Working with clients of all ages and fitness levels over the past two decades has taught me many valuable lessons. Those experiences definitely shaped my outlook on healthy weight loss and overall fitness.

While working as an active rehab specialist in a physiotherapy clinic several years ago, I came across patients who were unable to participate in the standard workout protocol. Lifting weights, jogging on a treadmill or jumping up and down were just not an option. So I resorted to walking. Whenever they came for their appointment, we went outside for a walk. At the beginning we would walk for 20 minutes and then gradually work our way to a full 60-minute session.

It didn't take long to see the outstanding benefits. Not only for my clients, but also for myself!

Results over time include:

- Overweight people reach their optimal weight
- Out of shape people attain maximum fitness
- Patients recover from injuries
- A reduction of high blood pressure
- Reduced stress, anxiety and depression

Personally, I can report that after including walking in my regular daily routine I have found:

- Increased energy
- Fewer aches and pains (especially in my lower back)
- Better quality sleep
- Improved mood and overall feeling of happiness :)

YOUR WEEK 1 FITNESS ASSIGNMENT

SIT LESS

Walk 20 minutes a day for five days this week. If you are already exercising, do the walks in addition to your regular workouts.

Your schedule can look something like this:

YOUR WEEK #1 fitness schedule*

*arrange walks and workouts as needed to fit appropriately into your schedule.

MONDAY	TUESDAY	WEDNESDAY	THURSDAY	FRIDAY	SATURDAY	SUNDAY
WALK 20 minutes	**WALK** 20 minutes		**WALK** 20 minutes	**WALK** 20 minutes	**WALK** 20 minutes	

My suggestion is to walk outside, even if you are in the city. If you have access to a beach, the forest or the mountains, take advantage of it!

Aim for getting your heart rate up. Include some hills and change up the pace to get a good sweat on.

Don't let the weather stop you from completing this challenge! Dress appropriately. In the worst-case scenario, you can walk in the shopping mall or at the gym on a treadmill.

Make sure to wear comfortable shoes. Find out how to choose the right shoe for you at www.activevegetarian.com.

I have days when I prefer walking alone, just listening to the sounds of nature. Other times, I ask a friend or a client to join me. If I'm in the city, I often put my headphones on and pass the time listening to an audiobook or podcast.

Think about how you are going to include this activity in your week—when and where are you going to walk?

LIFESTYLE

> "People often say that motivation doesn't last. Well, neither does bathing—that's why we recommend it daily."
>
> —Zig Ziglar

If there is something most of us have in common, it would be a desire to make our lives better. We might have different goals and dreams, but at the core, we all want positive change. So why is it that some people arrive at their goals, while others just can't find the will to finish what they started?

As far as we know, motivation is the answer to that question. Motivation can be hard to find, especially on a daily basis.

Perhaps this is not your first attempt at losing weight and getting healthy. Maybe you have tried before and at the beginning of a new weight-loss program, things were pretty exciting. The idea of a change got you all fired up!

You were motivated to exercise and it seemed pretty easy to stay away from junk foods. Making healthy choices felt effortless.

But then, a few weeks into it, things started to take a different turn. Your motivation slowly faded away and you hit a rough patch. You skipped a few workouts, ordered pizza for dinner and all of sudden life took you offtrack. All those efforts you had put in up until that point suddenly seemed to dissipate.

If that sounds familiar, it's okay—pretty much everyone who sets out on a new journey of cleaning up their diet, reducing processed foods and starting to exercise regularly will at some point or another run into a similar scenario.

Here is the honest truth: Things are going to suck sometimes. That's the reality of life. You're going to have moments of weakness when you want nothing more than a bag of chips, a burger and fries or a glazed doughnut. There will be days when you have to drag yourself out of the house for your scheduled walk.

Your mind might create thoughts like, "It's just this one time" or "I'm really tired today" or "I had a stressful day at work and I deserve a break."

But hold on! It doesn't have to spiral into a deep, dark hole. Just because you got offtrack for a split second doesn't mean the journey is over!

I have been fortunate to have a rewarding career in the health and fitness field. Over the past two decades, I have tested several ways to keep my personal motivation strong as well as help others realize their goals.

I believe that I have succeeded and found what really works. Here I share it with you, so you, too, can set yourself up for success and reach your desired goal.

I KNOW WHAT I WANT . . .

I wish I could take full credit for this concept, but it was Napoleon Hill who introduced me to the following four steps to success. Napoleon Hill's teachings have positively impacted millions of people around the world. I believe that you can benefit from it, too. After applying the following four steps to my life, I have gained a clear understanding of what I truly desire and what I am willing to give up in order to achieve my goals. This understanding has helped me to overcome obstacles along the way, pulled me out of a slump when things got rough and ultimately guided me to success. I hope you will find these steps helpful along your own journey.

Motivation is not magic. It does not come in a bottle. We need to nourish it and give it some love and attention in order to keep the flame burning. You are absolutely capable of accomplishing your goals and desires, so don't sell yourself short. Dream big and take action.

YOUR WEEK 1 LIFESTYLE ASSIGNMENT

THE KEY TO ENDLESS MOTIVATION

Get a notebook or print out the Mission Statement Worksheet from www.activevegetarian.com and let's begin . . .

STEP #1

At the beginning of any journey, it's crucial to decide on your desired outcome. In Part I of this book, we asked you to answer one question: "What would you like to gain from this eight-week plan?" Do you remember? If you haven't done so yet, here is another opportunity. You can do it now. We encourage you to take this assignment seriously. In this exercise, you will be asked to contemplate what it is that you really want out of this eight-week journey. There could be a number of whys. Note the ones that move you and inspire you and write them down in your notebook. Your why has to be big enough to pull you through those rough patches. Allow yourself to dream big and be as detailed as possible.

Here are few examples to get you inspired:

Why do I want this?

- I want to lose 10 pounds (4.5 kg) and become energized.
- I want to have enough energy to be a good mom/dad.
- I want a healthier body: heart, muscles, mind, skin, etc.
- I want to learn how to live a healthy life and thrive.
- I want to feel confident in my own skin.
- I want to be good example for my family/friends/ partner.
- And so on . . .

Remember that your only limitations are the ones you build in your own mind. Don't be afraid to aim high!

STEP #2

Now it's time to decide what you are willing to do in order to achieve this. "There ain't no such thing as a free lunch." Before we can enjoy our reward, we need to pay the price for it.

That's just how life works.

During this journey, you will learn valuable lessons and that will make the reward even more worth it—we can promise you that!

In your notebook, underneath your "why," write down the price you are willing to pay.

It could look something like this:

- I will stay committed and complete this eight-week plan.
- I will rid my kitchen of all junk food and only buy healthy foods from now on.
- I will put aside time to properly plan and prepare my meals.
- I will dedicate 20 to 60 minutes each day to exercise.
- I will give up my regular pizza nights with friends.
- I will drink more water and give up soda/pop.
- I will not quit; instead, I'll look at failure as a stepping stone to success.
- I will work toward my goals every single day.
- And so on . . .

Come up with as many things you are willing to change as possible. The higher the price you pay, the sweeter the reward. But it has to be genuine, as you will have to be able to back it up with appropriate action!

STEP #3

In your notebook, we want you to compose a clear commitment statement.

The previous two steps are crucial for step three to take place. What you wrote down so far—the whys and the price you are willing to pay—form a clear statement of your commitment. We often fear the word **commitment**, yet the truth is that without commitment, there is no chance for lasting success.

For this formula to work in your favor, it's important to read it out loud every single day. If you are super committed to your health goals, I suggest you keep your statement by your bed and read it twice per day—once in the morning as soon as you wake up and last thing at night before you rest your eyes.

Your statement could look something like this:

"My mission is to get fit and healthy for life. I am ready to enjoy life and feel good in my own body. I want to be proud of the way I look as well as what I can do. I want to lead by example and inspire the people in my life to eat healthy and exercise. I will accomplish this by following the eight-week *Vegan Weight Loss Manifesto* program. I will complete all outlined weekly assignments and instill the habits necessary to lose the weight and learn how to maintain my new fit and healthy body. I am open to including purposeful methods in my life, so that I can learn how to cope with stress and understand the power of positive thinking. I am ready to dedicate myself and make my health and well-being a priority."

Read your statement every single day until your desires (your whys) become your reality.

How will this daily habit benefit you?

It is estimated that we experience about 50,000 thoughts every day. By identifying your desire and your willingness to reach it, you allow your brain to focus on this specific purpose for your life.

Instead of drifting and allowing outside influences to fill your mind with self-destructive thoughts, you are now directing your attention and moving closer to a healthier, happier you!

STEP #4

Every day, take as many actions as possible that get you closer to your goal and minimize the things that set you back.

Writing things down and reading them daily is important, but without taking the appropriate action, you won't get too far. From now on, make a commitment to take all the steps necessary. The beauty of this eight-week plan is that we provide you with a step-by-step breakdown. Even if you are not sure yet how to implement these action steps, that's okay. With every new week you will learn strategies and adopt healthy habits necessary to succeed. All you have to do is your part—get the work done.

WEEK 1 RESOURCES AVAILABLE FOR YOU AT WWW.ACTIVEVEGETARIAN.COM

- Week #1 Meal Plan
- Shopping List (printable PDF)
- Meal Planning Template (printable PDF)
- "When to Buy Organic?" (article)
- "Shift to a Vegan Lifestyle" Part 1 (audio)
- "The Ultimate Guide to Plant-Based Nutrition" with Julieanna Hever, M.S., R.D., C.P.T. (audio interview)
- How to Choose Your Shoes (video)
- Mission Statement Worksheet

week #1 **MEAL PLAN**

MONDAY

MEAL #1 (Between 6am - 8am)	IMMUNE BOOSTER	PAGE 71
MEAL #2 (Between 8am - 10am)	ONE PIECE OF FRUIT (apple)	PAGE 19
MEAL #3 (Between 10am - 12pm)	CHICKPEA SALAD SANDWICH	PAGE 101
MEAL #4 (Between 12pm - 3pm)	ONE NO BAKE FIG CRUMB BAR	PAGE 145
MEAL #5 (Between 5pm - 8pm)	KITCHARI with BASIC GREEN SALAD	PAGE 125, 91

TUESDAY

MEAL #1 (Between 6am - 8am)	GLOWING GREEN	PAGE 67
MEAL #2 (Between 8am - 10am)	ONE NO BAKE FIG CRUMB BAR	PAGE 145
MEAL #3 (Between 10am - 12pm)	KITCHARI with 2 cups FRESH VEGGIES (carrots/cucumber/peppers)	PAGE 125
MEAL #4 (Between 12pm - 3pm)	ONE PIECE OF FRUIT (orange)	PAGE 19
MEAL #5 (Between 5pm - 8pm)	COLLARD WRAPS filled with CHICKPEA SALAD	PAGE 138, 101

WEDNESDAY

MEAL #1 (Between 6am - 8am)	EVERYONE'S FAVORITE	PAGE 64
MEAL #2 (Between 8am - 10am)	OVERNIGHT MAPLE WALNUT OATS	PAGE 83
MEAL #3 (Between 10am - 12pm)	BASIC GREEN SALAD	PAGE 91
MEAL #4 (Between 12pm - 3pm)	MATCHA LATTE	PAGE 73
MEAL #5 (Between 5pm - 8pm)	HEARTY LENTIL STEW	PAGE 116

THURSDAY

MEAL #1 (Between 6am - 8am)	BODYBUILDER	PAGE 63
MEAL #2 (Between 8am - 10am)	TWO CARDAMOM GINGER BLISS BALLS	PAGE 146
MEAL #3 (Between 10am - 12pm)	HEARTY LENTIL STEW	PAGE 116
MEAL #4 (Between 12pm - 3pm)	ONE PIECE OF FRUIT (1 cup of berries)	PAGE 19
MEAL #5 (Between 5pm - 8pm)	ZOODLES with SUN-DRIED TOMATO BASIL SAUCE	PAGE 105

FRIDAY

MEAL #1 (Between 6am - 8am)	BLUEBERRY PIE	PAGE 68
MEAL #2 (Between 8am - 10am)	ONE PIECE OF FRUIT (apple)	PAGE 19
MEAL #3 (Between 10am - 12pm)	ROASTED RED PEPPER SANDWICH with BASIC GREEN SALAD	PAGE 93, 91
MEAL #4 (Between 12pm - 3pm)	ONE NO BAKE FIG CRUMB BAR	PAGE 145
MEAL #5 (Between 5pm - 8pm)	KITCHARI with BASIC GREEN SALAD	PAGE 125, 91

SATURDAY

MEAL #1 (Between 6am - 8am)	RISE AND SHINE	PAGE 63
MEAL #2 (Between 8am - 10am)	ZOATS	PAGE 84
MEAL #3 (Between 10am - 12pm)	CHEEZY BROCCOLI SOUP	PAGE 112
MEAL #4 (Between 12pm - 3pm)	ONE PIECE OF FRUIT (orange)	PAGE 19
MEAL #5 (Between 5pm - 8pm)	COLLARD WRAPS filled with CHICKPEA SALAD	PAGE 183, 101

SUNDAY

MEAL #1 (Between 6am - 8am)	PURITY	PAGE 64
MEAL #2 (Between 8am - 10am)	THE ULTIMATE VEGAN BREAKFAST SANDWICH	PAGE 87
MEAL #3 (Between 10am - 12pm)	BASIC GREEN SALAD	PAGE 91
MEAL #4 (Between 12pm - 3pm)	ONE FIVE-INGREDIENT PROTEIN BAR	PAGE 142
MEAL #5 (Between 5pm - 8pm)	CHICKPEA & RATATOUILLE	PAGE 129

WEEK 2

NUTRITION

"Water is the driver of nature."

—Leonardo da Vinci

You probably already know that you are supposed to drink water, but according to new research, up to 75 percent of North Americans are functioning in a chronic state of dehydration.[2]

Now that's crazy. It's crazy because a lot of health issues that are treated with medications could easily be fixed or even avoided if people just made sure to drink enough clean water.

Why is water so important for our overall health? Our bodies are composed of up to 50 to 75 percent water; all that water is absolutely essential for your well-being and your body needs it for pretty much every function. Water carries oxygen and nutrients, transports hormones, moistens tissues, protects organs, regulates body temperature, lubricates joints and helps to eliminate toxins through the colon, skin and bladder.

So if you are one of the 75 percent of people who are chronically dehydrated, you might experience symptoms such as:

- Fatigue and energy loss
- Difficulty concentrating
- Joint pain
- Constipation
- Digestive disorders
- High or low blood pressure
- Gastritis, stomach ulcers
- Respiratory troubles
- Excess weight and obesity
- Insomnia
- Eczema, acne
- Premature aging

- Anxiety and depression
- Slow metabolism
- And many more . . .

The bottom line is that we need water to be healthy, happy and fit!

WHAT ELSE CAN I DRINK?

What if I don't like water, can I drink juice or soda instead?

NO! Ditch the calorie-containing drinks. In fact, all of your drinks should come from non-calorie containing beverages. Fruit juice, alcoholic drinks, coffee, tea and sodas (diet soda included) don't count! In fact, most of these should be removed from your daily menu. For hydration, stick with water. If you do drink tea or coffee, try to drink it black or with a splash of nondairy milk. Green tea is also a nice choice. However, tea and coffee don't count as part of your daily water intake.

Drink Plenty of Clean Water

I want to put the emphasis on CLEAN water. Today's tap water is nothing short of scary. In most parts of North America, we are lucky to have access to running water. The trouble is that this water is often mass-produced. Unfortunately, water treatment means adding hormone-disrupting chemicals like chlorine, man-made fluoride and an assortment of heavy metals. [3]

Common Contaminants in Tap Water Include:[4]

- Toilet paper residue (yes, you are reading that right!)
- Heavy metals such as lead, cadmium and arsenic
- Pesticide runoff
- Petrochemicals
- Residues of pharmaceutical medications such as birth control, antidepressants, etc.

Your body recognizes all these chemicals as poison and has to filter them. This puts unnecessary strain on our bodies.

---

3   http://www.cbc.ca/news/health/drinking-water-contaminated-by-excreted-drugs-a-growing-concern-1.2772289

4   David Wolfe. 2013. *Longevity Now: A Comprehensive Approach to Healthy Hormones, Detoxification, Super Immunity, Reversing Calcification, and Total Rejuvenation.* North Atlantic Books. Pg.153

---

2   Michelle Cederberg. 2012. *Energy Now!: Small Steps to an Energetic Life.* Sentient Publications. Pg.129

So, what can YOU do?

Drink and use ONLY pure water! This could mean:

- An under-the-counter water filtration system
- Spring water (in glass bottles) regularly delivered to your home
- Going out and foraging your own

YOUR WEEK 2 NUTRITION ASSIGNMENT

STAY PROPERLY HYDRATED

- Ditch the unhealthy drinks.
- Stop drinking chlorinated tap water and start drinking clean water!
- Find a way to get purified water into your home (filters, water delivery, find and purify your own—www.findaspring.com).
- Download a handy water tracking chart at www.activevegetarian.com.

HOW MUCH DO YOU NEED?

While it's hard to exactly determine an ideal amount, we have some guidelines[5] you can follow:

- Men should drink about 13 cups (3.1 L) of total fluids a day.
- Women should drink about 9 cups (2.2 L) of total fluids a day.

Men need a little more because they tend to be larger on average and naturally have more muscle mass—which holds water better than fatty tissues. Of course, pregnant women and nursing mothers need more water as well.

FITNESS

Recently I came across an article on CNN's website with this headline:

"Sitting Will Kill You, Even if You Exercise"[6]

Sounds pretty extreme, wouldn't you say? However, this statement starts to make some sense once we look closer and acknowledge some of the lifestyle changes that have taken place around us in the past 100 years.

Here is a biology bit for you: Our body has more than 200 bones and more than 600 skeletal muscles that allow us to move and perform various tasks.

In order for the body to keep functioning in an optimal way, it needs movement. What will happen to a car if it's not being driven? It will start to deteriorate, no doubt about it. Your body is very much the same. Those muscles and bones will start to crumble if they don't get the right form of movement. That old saying "move it or lose it" is a perfect way to put it.

Today, many of us live in a world where most things surrounding us can be managed by the touch of a button.

This ever-increasing ability to rely on technology is perhaps making things faster and more convenient, but it comes with an unfortunate side effect.

Just think about how much time we spend sitting down. When we drive, we sit. When we work at an office, we sit. When we watch TV, read, eat, meet someone for a coffee . . . well, you get the picture.

While a brief period of sitting here and there is natural, long periods of sitting day in and day out can seriously impact your health and shorten your life.

The reason is simple. The human body never holds on to something it does not use.

If we do not move our bodies enough, our skeletal muscles will diminish and our joints will get stiff. But loss of muscle mass and aching knees are not the only side effects of a sedentary lifestyle. Moving our bodies also helps to maintain the health of our internal organs—it massages them gently. If we move our bodies regularly, we will be able to maintain normal body weight, reduce the possibility of heart disease, diabetes, cancer and digestion problems and regain mental clarity and prolong life.

YOUR WEEK 2 FITNESS ASSIGNMENT

MOVE MORE

- Increase your walks to 25 minutes at least five times this week.
- Move more. Incorporate movement into your life and your job, whenever and wherever you can.

Your schedule can look something like this:

---

5 http://www.dietitians.ca/Your-Health/Nutrition-A-Z/Water/Why-is-water-so-important-for-my-body---Know-when-.aspx

6 http://www.cnn.com/2015/01/21/health/sitting-will-kill-you/

YOUR WEEK #2 fitness schedule*

*arrange walks and workouts as needed to fit appropriately into your schedule.

MONDAY	TUESDAY	WEDNESDAY	THURSDAY	FRIDAY	SATURDAY	SUNDAY
WALK 25 minutes	**WALK** 25 minutes		**WALK** 25 minutes	**WALK** 25 minutes	**WALK** 25 minutes	

Use the following strategies as often as possible:

Move-More Ideas for Work

1. Park far away and take the stairs.

2. Make phone calls while pacing, rather than sitting down.

3. Walk to a coworker's desk instead of emailing or calling.

4. Stand up and move whenever you have a drink of water at work.

5. Visit the restroom on a different floor and take the stairs.

6. Go for a walk outside during your lunch break.

7. Walk briskly when heading to meetings.

8. Instead of booking a conference room, have "walking meetings" at work when meeting with small groups.

We realize how easy it is to get lost in your work and forget to move. While writing this book, we played around with different sitting positions and found ways to stand and work, but one thing that helped a lot was setting a timer to remind us to move. Simply set a reminder alarm on your phone or computer that goes off every hour and don't ignore it. Take at least a five-minute break. During this time, you can walk, stand or take the opportunity to do a few simple exercises by your desk.

For a video demonstrating simple exercises as well as great alternatives to sitting in a chair, go to www.activevegetarian.com.

Move-More Ideas for Daily Life

1. Go for a family walk after dinner.

2. Walk or bike to your destination instead of driving.

3. Get a pedometer and start tracking your steps. Progress up to 10,000 steps or more a day.

4. Play outside with your kids.

5. Walk or run as your kids ride their bikes.

6. Instead of sitting, walk around while watching your child's sporting event.

7. Take a walk when you are frustrated or bored (instead of eating).

8. Go for a walk with a friend instead of meeting for coffee.

9. Turn on the music and dance around the house.

10. Take your dog for a walk (if you already do this, try making the walk longer or faster).

11. Walk through your golf game instead of driving a cart.

12. Walk up and down escalators instead of just riding them.

13. Try standing and moving whenever you are talking on a cellphone.

LIFESTYLE

"Early to bed and early to rise makes a man healthy, wealthy and wise."

—*Benjamin Franklin*

Sleep is just as important as nutrition and exercise when it comes to improving your health, losing weight and gaining an overall feeling of awesomeness.

Getting a good night's sleep will not only help your body recover but is also crucial for your emotional health, keeping you happy and mentally focused.

On the other hand, recurring nights of bad sleep will pile on body fat, mess with your hormones, make you more susceptible to chronic illnesses, steal your energy and drain your spirit.

Anyone who has experienced a few nights of lousy sleep knows what we're talking about. Fortunately, I am a pretty good sleeper, but on the rare occasions when something interferes with my nighttime rest (mostly long-distance travel) I feel totally out of balance the following day. My brain feels fuzzy and slow, my mood is unpredictable, my skin doesn't look fresh (not to mention those bags under my eyes), I feel incredibly hungry yet my metabolism is super slow, my productivity drops and I come up with million excuses to avoid exercise. Now imagine dealing with this day after day . . . That's no fun and definitely not healthy!

Let's just look at few other risks associated with sleepless nights:[7]

- Increased risk of diabetes
- Increased risk of some cancers
- Increased risk of heart disease
- Risk of stroke quadruples
- Increased hunger and weight gain
- Increase in memory problems/more likely to have an accident
- Loss of brain tissue
- Lower sex drive and decreased sperm count

Scary stuff, huh?

Fortunately, research also shows that returning to adequate sleep can quickly improve the way you feel and reduce these risks. That's why this week's focus will be on getting that replenishing shut-eye.

YOUR WEEK 2 LIFESTYLE ASSIGNMENT

CREATE A BEDTIME RITUAL

A bedtime ritual is an awesome way to get kids ready for bed and create the right atmosphere for a good night's rest. So why should adults be any different?

For the next seven days, develop the following three habits:

Get to bed by 10 p.m.

Most of us focus on how many hours of sleep we get. However, it's not just the quantity of sleep—what's more important is the quality.

The deepest and most regenerative sleep occurs between 10 p.m. and 2 a.m.

Your adrenals function best to recharge your body during these hours and this is also when your body is geared up for its peak internal cleansing and rejuvenation cycle. You will wake feeling lighter, fresher, more energetic and positive.

Switch off the electronic devices at least 30 minutes before bed.

Whether it's a TV, computer or phone, unplug from all devices.

No more stimulating your brain this late at night. Checking your emails and browsing social media can be addictive and often keeps us up longer. Also, the light from all these devices will interfere with a restful sleep.

Read something light or listen to soothing music.

I like to let my mind wander through some pages in the evening. Nothing stressful or too involved, like a nice light book. Nikki prefers listening to some mellow music as a way to relax the body and mind before bed. She says, "It's perfect! I start my playlist (which is available on our website), select a sleep timer, plug in my headphones and start to drift off."

WEEK 2 RESOURCES AVAILABLE FOR YOU ON WWW.ACTIVEVEGETARIAN.COM:

- Week #2 Meal Plan and Shopping List
- "Benefits of Drinking More Water" (article)
- Water Tracking Chart (printable PDF)
- Shift to a Vegan Lifestyle Part 2 (audio)
- A Guide to Chair Alternatives for Sitting at a Desk (video)
- Nikki's Bedtime Playlist (audio)

---

7   Patel, Sanjay R., and Frank B. Hu, "Short Sleep Duration and Weight Gain: A Systematic Review," North American Association for the Study of Obesity (2008), doi: 10.1038/oby.2007.118.

WEEK 3

NUTRITION

"The food you eat can be either the safest and most powerful form of medicine or the slowest form of poison."

—Ann Wigmore

By now your kitchen should be free from any junk and processed stuff and fully stocked with healthy, real plant-based food. Also, you are on point with drinking 9 to 13 cups (2.2 to 3.1 L) of water every single day. If this statement is correct—great! You're ready to move on.

On the other hand, if you haven't completed those assigned tasks from the previous two weeks, we strongly suggest you revisit them.

We don't care if it takes you a full month to complete those weekly assignments, as long as you do the best you can and give it 100 percent each day.

Remember what we said at the beginning in the section "How to Get the Most Out of This Book" (page 11)?

The only way you'll form long-lasting habits is by focusing on one thing at a time. This way you'll be able to focus all your energy on that one habit and creating a permanent positive change.

YOUR WEEK 3 NUTRITION ASSIGNMENT

HOW MUCH, WHEN AND WHAT?

Just because you're on a vegan diet doesn't automatically mean you're a healthy eater. This week you will focus on:

- What to eat (and drink)
- When to eat it
- How much to eat

WHAT'S ON MY PLATE?

We want to focus on:

- Green leafy vegetables and fresh herbs (one-fourth of your plate): kale, spinach, mustard greens, collard greens, Swiss chard, arugula, micro greens, romaine lettuce, basil, parsley, cilantro

- Other vegetables (one-fourth of your plate): all kinds, including carrots, beets, broccoli, cauliflower, summer and winter squash, cabbage

- Healthy fats (one-sixth of your plate): avocado, sprouted nuts and seeds, hemp oil, flax oil, coconut oil

- Whole grains (one-sixth of your plate): quinoa, sprouted-grain bread, oats

- Sprouts and legumes (one-sixth of your plate): alfalfa, chickpeas, mung beans, lentils, adzuki beans, green peas

- Fruit: all kinds, fresh, in season, as a snack (on an empty stomach)

- Water: clean, room temperature

OTHER NOTES

- Eat slowly and stop when 80 percent full
- Choose local and organic foods whenever possible
- Choose whole non-processed foods

Q: Do I need to count calories?

A: No. Don't worry about counting calories. Monitor your results and if needed, adjust the size of your plate.

A word about fruit:

Every time I eat watermelon I burp; when I eat an apple my stomach bloats up; when I eat a banana I feel like running to the toilet . . . those are very common complaints we get from clients. Perhaps you've also experienced a similar issue. This is not a reason to avoid eating fruit! Fruit is healthy for you; it should be a part of your diet! However, in order to get the full health benefits and avoid any digestive troubles, it's advisable to follow some general guidelines.

Let's say you eat a peanut butter sandwich (not recommended, by the way) and then a slice of fruit. The slice of fruit takes no time to digest and is ready to go straight through the stomach into the intestines.

What's On My Plate?

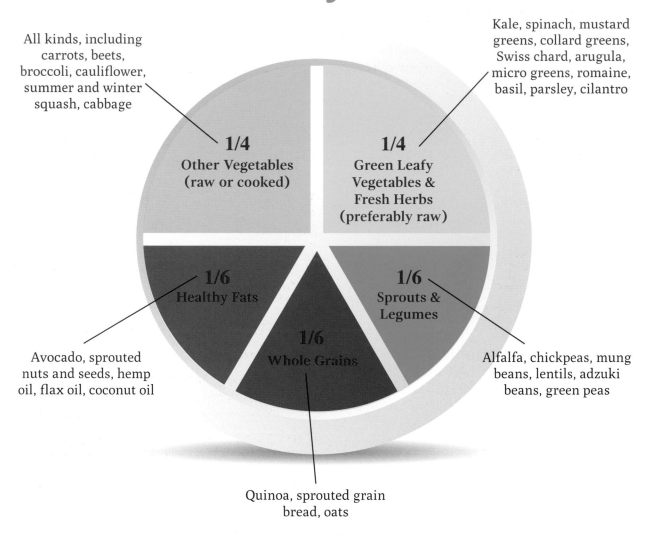

All kinds, including carrots, beets, broccoli, cauliflower, summer and winter squash, cabbage

Kale, spinach, mustard greens, collard greens, Swiss chard, arugula, micro greens, romaine, basil, parsley, cilantro

1/4
Other Vegetables
(raw or cooked)

1/4
Green Leafy
Vegetables &
Fresh Herbs
(preferably raw)

1/6
Healthy Fats

1/6
Sprouts &
Legumes

1/6
Whole Grains

Avocado, sprouted nuts and seeds, hemp oil, flax oil, coconut oil

Alfalfa, chickpeas, mung beans, lentils, adzuki beans, green peas

Quinoa, sprouted grain bread, oats

Water: Clean, room temperature

Fruit: All kinds, fresh, in season

TIPS
- Eat slowly and stop when 80 percent full
- Choose local and organic foods whenever possible
- Choose whole non-processed foods

Unfortunately, that bread and peanut butter you just consumed takes much longer to process and it is preventing the fruit from passing through your digestive tract.

What ends up happening is the whole meal of sandwich and fruit rots and ferments and turns to acid. The minute the fruit comes into contact with the other food in the stomach and digestive juices, the entire mass of food begins to spoil, which can cause bloating, gas and indigestion.[8]

For that reason, we suggest that you eat fruit either on an empty stomach, first thing in the morning, or as midday snack. Making a fresh juice out of fruit and vegetables is also a wonderful way to receive their benefits. Another option is to experiment with mixing fruit such as berries or oranges into your green salad and monitor how your body reacts.

MEAL FREQUENCY

Our meal plans are based on five meals per day.

MONDAYfood PROTOCOL

MEAL #1 (Between 6am - 8am)	NAME OF RECIPE	PAGE xx
MEAL #2 (Between 8am - 10am)	Deep Chocolate Milk	PAGE xx
MEAL #3 (Between 10am - 12pm)	NAME OF RECIPE	PAGE xx
MEAL #4 (Between 12pm - 3pm)	NAME OF RECIPE	PAGE xx
MEAL #5 (Between 5pm - 8pm)	NAME OF RECIPE	PAGE xx

Full-Day Food Protocol

Meal #1 (Between 6 a.m. and 8 a.m.)

Meal #2 (Between 8 a.m. and 10 a.m.)

Meal #3 (Between 10 a.m. and noon)

Meal #4 (Between noon and 3 p.m.)

Meal #5 (Between 5 p.m. and 8 p.m.)

HOW MUCH TO EAT

- Eat only when you are hungry.
- Eat until satisfied, instead of stuffed ("80 percent full feeling").
- Eat slowly and mindfully, without distraction.
- Our recipes yield one to four servings. Keep that in mind when portioning your meals.

---

8   International Wellness Directory. "How To Eat Fruit Correctly," last modified 2010, http://www.mnwelldir.org/docs/misc/fruit_debunk.htm.

For weekly meal plans to help you stay on track, go to www.activevegetarian.com.

FITNESS

"I just wish people would realize that anything's possible if you try."

—Terry Fox

Our hope is that you are already regularly enjoying your walks and your body is feeling stronger and fitter than two weeks ago.

We are aware that a few of you might currently be experiencing some sort of physical pain. Perhaps you are trying to ignore it and power through or maybe this pain is completely stopping you from your regular exercise.

Well, guess what? We have some good news: There's always a way to work around an injury and build a healthy, strong and lean body. This week you will learn how.

HOW TO GET IN SHAPE, EVEN WITH AN INJURY

Here are five key steps:

1. Don't ignore an injury!

Often we feel that if we don't do anything, skip exercise and rest, it will get better on its own. But that is a big mistake!

If you don't do anything to promote healing, it can get much worse. Your body will compensate and what started as pain in the knee could lead to a sore back, aching shoulder or recurring headaches.

2. Ask for help.

Get a professional diagnosis. Depending on the type of pain or injury, consult your doctor, physiotherapist, chiropractor or massage therapist. Get their okay to carry on with regular exercise or ask for suggestions on how to heal. A good therapist should not only help ease the pain but also provide a solution to strengthen any weak areas and prevent further troubles.

It might also be a good idea to hire a personal trainer, so he or she can observe your form while exercising. And yes, we are even talking about walking! You would be surprised by how many people don't walk correctly, causing more harm than good.

3. Proper nutrition is the key to helping your body heal.

Now it's more important than ever to properly nourish your body and apply all the lessons you have learned so far. That means staying away from processed foods, fast food, packaged food and anything containing sugar and artificial sweeteners, including regular and diet soda or pop.

All these foods will cause unnecessary inflammation in the body, which will prevent healing from taking place.

Instead, focus on eating fresh, preferably organic vegetables, fruit and whole sprouted grains. Don't forget to include plenty of healthy fats, such as flax oil, hemp oil, extra virgin olive oil, avocado and soaked nuts and seeds. Stay hydrated with clean, fresh water.

4. Supplement.

Rather than relying on anti-inflammatory drugs such as Advil or Motrin, consider trying one of these herbs: turmeric, ginger and bromeliad (not an herb, but an enzyme found in pineapple). All these have been known for centuries to be the most powerful natural healers.

5. Stay active.

One of the worst things you can do when you get hurt is to completely eliminate all physical activity. Resting the affected area and proper sleep are crucial to a good recovery. But this doesn't mean that you need to become a couch potato.

Unless you are in a body cast or lying in a hospital bed, there is absolutely no reason why you can't work around an injury. Perhaps you have been given some exercises by your physical therapist. If so, make sure you do them together with this week's fitness assignment.

No matter what, don't give up! Many of our clients have serious health limitations when they start working with us. And yes, they've considered giving up too. But after losing 10, 20 or 30 pounds (4.5, 9 or 13.6 kg) of unhealthy body weight, they're transformed.

YOUR WEEK 3 FITNESS ASSIGNMENT

MOBILITY MATTERS

Continue with your 25-minute walk at least 5 times this week.

Perform Mobility Session 3 times this week.

Follow along with our Mobility Session video available at www.activevegetarian.com.

Your schedule can look something like this:

YOUR WEEK #3 fitness schedule*

*arrange walks, workouts and mobility sessions as needed to fit appropriately into your schedule.

MONDAY	TUESDAY	WEDNESDAY	THURSDAY	FRIDAY	SATURDAY	SUNDAY
WALK 25 minutes	**WALK** 25 minutes	**MOBILITY SESSION** 15 minutes	**WALK** 25 minutes	**WALK** 25 minutes + **MOBILITY SESSION** 15 minutes	**WALK** 25 minutes	**MOBILITY SESSION** 15 minutes

LIFESTYLE

A few years back, martial arts were a big part of my daily life. It started in my early twenties and carried on for about ten years. During that period of time, I would train, help around the studio and later also teach classes. I basically lived martial arts!

I still have the Student Creed deeply engraved in my mind:

> *"Watch your thoughts, they become words; watch your words, they become actions; watch your actions, they become habits; watch your habits, they become character; watch your character, for it becomes your destiny."*

Students were asked to memorize and recite these words before each class. It was our little mantra. And as with any mantra, if repeated over and over enough times, it leaves a permanent imprint on your mind. This impression, if strong enough, has the power to help us make those positive statements come alive.

Once in a while I come across someone's Facebook post or Instagram feed that reads, "Your thoughts create your life" or "You are what you think." Yes, to some degree it's correct, but while our thoughts are a part of what creates reality, they are not the only mover. However, your thoughts are where your reality originates. For that reason, it's important to pay attention to what goes on in your mind.

Just like the student creed says: "Thoughts to words to actions to habits to character, we arrive at our destiny."

EMOTIONAL EATING AND WEIGHT LOSS

What does all this have to do with weight loss, you might ask . . . well, a lot! To experience permanent positive change in any area of your life, whether it's your health, relationships or career, it all begins with a single thought. Your life today is a direct reflection of your thoughts.

Sound a little too New Agey to you? Let's make this more real, rather than just theoretical. Let's use an example. Let's talk about "Kim."

Kim had a great childhood. Although she was an only child, she never felt alone growing up in a big Italian family. Since all the relatives enjoyed frequent get-togethers, there was never a lack of cousins to play with. There was also never a lack of food around, as that played a big part of the entertainment. Kim was encouraged to eat as much as she wanted and was praised every time she finished her fully loaded plate.

During her early teens, her dad's company moved the family across the country. Not long after that, the family dynamic started to change. Arguments between Kim's parents were escalating and it was obvious that there were troubles in the marriage.

Not having friends or relatives around, Kim often felt very lonely and abandoned. She was searching for something to relieve her sadness. Food was the obvious choice. After all, just thinking of food would bring back those happy childhood feelings. Feelings of love and approval associated with food were so strong that eating became her therapy.

"All I wanted was for Mom and Dad to get back together. I felt like everything I'd known had been destroyed. When they split up, I took refuge in food. I ate and ate and ate. But still I couldn't fill the void."

Once you get on the roller coaster of emotional eating, it can be very difficult to get off. If you allow your thoughts of food as comfort to turn into actions and start to literally feed your void, you will create a strong, unhealthy habit. You can imagine what kind of damage this harmful pattern will manifest not only to your physical health but also to your emotional well-being.

Emotional eating creates a very sick relationship with food. It's just like a drug. Food provides the fun, entertainment, control, reassurance or love that's missing in someone's life. Food may also help to numb difficult emotions like fear and sadness.

If you are serious about changing your life, we really need you to be honest with yourself.

See if you relate to any of the following:

- Always trying a new diet
- Eating beyond fullness at dinner
- Snacking on junk food during the day to help deal with your job's stress
- Not eating enough and always worrying about getting fat
- Eating a couple of bags of chips while watching TV on Friday night
- Snacking all day to ease the boredom of an unsatisfying life

- Obsessed with perfection, never feeling happy with your body
- Suffering with nutrition-related disease (e.g., heart disease, diabetes, etc.) yet resisting lifestyle changes

NOW it's the time to stop allowing food to control your life!

Let's get serious and make a lasting change. Enough of this merry-go-round of losing and gaining weight. By paying attention to your thoughts, you gain the power to start overwriting those old patterns associated with food. This is your key to heal the pain and trauma and set yourself free.

YOUR WEEK 3 LIFESTYLE ASSIGNMENT

ONE-MINUTE MEDITATION

Most of our habitual behaviors, including the ones associated with food, happen automatically and without a lot of awareness. Our brains produce as many as 50,000 thoughts per day (according to the National Science Foundation). [9]

Out of these 50,000 thoughts, a majority—around 95 percent—are repeated thoughts and 70 to 80 percent are geared toward the negative! That's a whole bunch of unnecessary negative stinking thinking. That has to change! And the first step you can take is to become aware of your own thoughts.

To develop a kinder mind and help you deal with stress, sadness, fear, frustration or any other negative thoughts you might be experiencing, follow the simple steps behind the One-Minute Meditation.

This meditation can be done anywhere:

- Put your phone away and minimize any possible distractions.
- Sit in a comfortable position: spine long and rooting your sitting bones into the earth.
- Close your eyes.
- Through your nose, take a deep breath in . . . and then exhale it out through your nose.
  - At some point a thought will arise; recognize it, label it as "thinking" and return your attention to the breath.

---

9   Jagarnath, Krishna, *Real Secrets of Life!: Divine Guidance and Higher Spiritual Techniques for the Next Century* (Carlsbad: BalboaPress, 2014).

- Continue this deep breathing for at least 10 full breaths.
- Use this short but powerful technique anytime you feel overwhelmed with emotions. Meditation works wonders when done regularly. Aim for at least once per day.

WEEK 3 RESOURCES AVAILABLE FOR YOU ON WWW.ACTIVEVEGETARIAN.COM:

- Week #3 Meal Plan and Shopping List
- Are You an Emotional Eater? (audio)
- Mobility Matters #1 (video)
- One-Minute Guided Meditation (video)

WEEK 4

NUTRITION

"By failing to prepare, you are preparing to fail."
—*Benjamin Franklin*

Meal planning, or the lack thereof, could be the make-or-break moment of your successful weight loss. We found that there are two major reasons why adopting a habit of prepping your meals ahead will help you succeed.

For one, lack of planning leads to poor choices later on. Imagine coming to work each day with your own nutritious lunch, fresh fruit and a big jug of clean water. How much healthier would your life be? When lunchtime rolls around, rather than heading down to the nearest fast-food joint, battling the busy streets and crazy lines, you can take a stroll down to the park and enjoy a peaceful, healthy meal.

Second, having your meals figured out ahead of time saves you a lot of thinking. Remember last week when we talked about the crazy number of thoughts most of us deal with? We have about 50,000 thoughts per day on average, and the power these thoughts harness is great! Now imagine how many thoughts involve food. If you get proactive and prep your meals ahead of time, you will be able to eliminate a huge amount of food thoughts. This way you could spend less time thinking about food, and more time creating and living your dream life.

YOUR WEEK 4 NUTRITION ASSIGNMENT

MEAL PREP 101

This week we are going to create a food ritual, which simply means that you set aside a bit of time to prepare some healthy food in advance so that it's ready, available and convenient when you need it. Use the following two strategies to help keep you consistent and get you closer to your goals.

Sunday and Wednesday Ritual

We find that these two days work best for us, but you can choose any two days of the week you like.

For us, Sundays and Wednesdays tend to be less busy and we are able to devote time to this type of task. Sundays are also a time when we're usually thinking ahead to the upcoming week. Whatever two days you choose, set aside two to three hours to do the following:

STEP #1

Check your schedule for the next three to four days.

What are your days going to look like? Meetings? Kids' activities? Late nights? How many times will you be eating out or with family? Start to form a better idea of how you can fit healthy meals into the next few days ahead.

STEP #2

Put together a menu.

Create your daily meal plan. Don't be afraid to repeat the same meal choice several times during the next few days. This will drastically cut down on your prep time.

We have weekly meal plans available for you on www.activevegetarian.com. Or you can also use one of our printable PDFs to create a meal plan for yourself.

STEP #3

Build your own shopping list from your menu.

Our PDF shopping list will help you stay organized and be more efficient once you hit the grocery store. Having a list also keeps you away from the temptation of buying random junk food and other unhealthy things.

STEP #4

Hit the grocery store.

Stock up on what you need for all your meals. It's not a bad idea to consider grabbing a few extra "just in case" emergency items such as fresh fruit, a bag of premixed greens for salad, a box of dates or figs and even a can of chickpeas.

STEP #5

Once you are back home, start prepping and cooking.

- Prep veggies for snacks, smoothies/juices and meals. Slice carrots, apples, zucchini, celery, bell peppers, cucumbers or any vegetables you might need. Also wash and properly dry your greens (spinach, lettuce, kale, etc.).

- You can prep individual bags/jars with cut fruit and greens for your smoothies and juices. These can be stored in the refrigerator or freezer.

- Get your juicer out and get to work if fresh juice is a part of the plan. We personally like to drink our juice fresh straight from the press, but you could store fresh juices in closed glass containers in your refrigerator for up to three days (depending on the style of juicer you have). Read more on how to pick the right juicer for you on www.activevegetarian.com.

- Soak any nuts, beans, seeds or grains you will need for the week. Refer to "Soaking and Sprouting" on page 184.

- If almond milk is one of your choices, prepare the Basic Almond Milk recipe (page 71) with your pre-soaked nuts.

- Blend up any sauces, dressings or dips.

- Prep any snacks for the week—protein bars, bliss balls, roasted chickpeas or whatever you decided on.

- If you have a chia pudding on your menu, create the base. Don't forget to consider the number of servings you need.

- Do the same for overnight oats.

- Cook all legumes such as chickpeas, lentils and beans. If you are using canned, make sure to wash them thoroughly under running water, transfer to a glass container and store in the refrigerator for later.

- Cook or soak all your grains: brown rice, wild rice, buckwheat or quinoa.

- Cook any sweet potatoes, yams and/or squash.

- Now assemble some of your meal choices, portion them for the week, store your food in stackable containers and make them accessible in the refrigerator or freezer.

WHAT IF I DON'T HAVE TWO TO THREE HOURS TO PREP?

You don't have time? Really? Let me tell you the truth, if you are serious about getting healthy and creating a lasting change, you will find time for this. Perhaps look at cutting out some activities that are taking you further away from your goals, like going to the bar on the weekend, playing games or wasting time scrolling through others' lives on social media. If you are in a relationship or if you have children, include your loved ones and allow them to help you. Make it a fun family ritual.

If your schedule absolutely 100 percent won't allow for time in the kitchen, you can hire a healthy vegan meal delivery service. Google "healthy meal delivery" in your area and see what pops up.

Morning Ritual

Each morning, take the following steps to get armed with healthy meals for the day:

- Blend up your smoothie, get your juice ready or finish up your overnight oats/chia pudding.

- Mix up your salad, and pack your dressing in a separate container to avoid soggy greens.

- If you haven't done so already, portion out your other meals.

- Pack your fruit, bars, roasted chickpeas, etc. for snacks.

- Don't forget your water!

If you plan on eating any meals at home, double check that you have everything on hand for easy and quick prep.

After a few weeks of meal prep practice, you will find what works and what doesn't. Make this ritual your own. Be creative and have fun with it. And if you happen to find something that works well, please share it with us. We're sure others would love to hear about it.

FITNESS

"In every walk with nature one receives far more than he seeks."

—John Muir

For the past three weeks, you've been building your fitness endurance with your regular walks, and this week you are ready to include a new challenge. Don't worry, we aren't going to ask you to sign up for a marathon. But it's time to step up your fitness regime and build your stamina by heading out for a hike. If this sounds way out of your comfort zone, GREAT. Growth and improvement will only happen when we are taken out of our comfort zone.

TOP FIVE REASONS YOU SHOULD TRY HIKING THIS WEEKEND:

1. It's simple and cheap

Hiking (just like your walking) is a simple activity that doesn't cost much. All that is required to enjoy it is a good pair of shoes, plenty of water, some snacks and a positive mental attitude. In many ways, hiking has the power to transform your life and make you a happier person.

2. It brings balance

Getting out into the fresh air, away from the hustle of the city, the stuffy air in the office building and the buzzing coffee shops around town provides welcome relief to an often stressful and fast-paced life. A hike through a beautiful wooded area can calm your nerves, lift your spirits and allow you to recharge your energy.

3. It's healthy

Is it ever! Hiking is a great way to get a serious workout without putting too much pressure on your joints. Just one hour of hiking can burn well over 500 calories, depending on the level of incline and the weight of the backpack you're carrying. By including regular hikes as a way to stay physically active, you can potentially lose weight, reduce your risk of heart disease, decrease hypertension and slow the aging process.[10]

10　　Harvard Health Publications. "Walking: Your steps to health," August, 2009, http://www.health.harvard.edu/newsletter_article/Walking-Your-steps-to-health.

4. It gets you high

A high not associated with drugs, alcohol or going out to the clubs and staying up all night partying, hiking offers a surreal sense of accomplishment and an adrenaline rush. It increases your dopamine and serotonin levels (happy hormones) in a healthy way. Not only that, but you'll also gain a sense of deeper value for yourself and for Mother Nature and become a more confident person by challenging yourself.

5. It's forever

It always warms my heart to see so many seniors on the trail. They have a healthy glow about them and often a big smile on their face. Yes, perhaps it takes them longer to get up a mountain but who cares, right? Hiking is for anyone and if you have children, we encourage you to introduce them to the world of the outdoors. It's an activity that they'll be able to enjoy their whole life. And so can you!

We find that hiking nourishes the mind, body and soul in ways that are difficult to describe. You just have to experience it for yourself and we urge you to try it this week.

YOUR WEEK 4 FITNESS ASSIGNMENT

TAKE A HIKE

- Continue with your 25-minute walk at least 4 times this week.
- Perform Mobility Session 3 times this week for 15 minutes.
- Include one hike in nature this week for 60 minutes or more.

Your schedule can look something like this:

A Few Safety Tips

- Avoid hiking alone—ask your spouse or a friend or join a group and together enjoy this adventure.
- Tell someone where you are going and when you will return.
- Stay on marked trails. No shortcuts or "bushwhacking"! This only increases your chance of becoming lost.
- Bring plenty of drinking water and some healthy snacks (fruit, homemade protein bars, bliss balls, etc.) and never assume stream water is safe to drink.
- Go onto www.alltrails.com to help you locate a trail/ hike in your area.
- Dress accordingly. The temperature is always cooler in the mountains. Wear layers.
- Pace yourself, enjoy the journey and breathe in the fresh air.

LIFESTYLE

"Nature does not hurry, yet everything is accomplished."

—*Lao Tzu*

We live hectic lives, doing what we can to keep up with this frantic pace of the world around us. The truth is that going faster doesn't necessarily equate with accomplishing more or performing better. Usually the exact opposite is true. Just like Lao Tzu states in his quote above, if you take the time to slow

YOUR WEEK #4 fitness schedule*

*arrange walks, workouts and mobility sessions as needed to fit appropriately into your schedule.

MONDAY	TUESDAY	WEDNESDAY	THURSDAY	FRIDAY	SATURDAY	SUNDAY
WALK 25 minutes	**WALK** 25 minutes + **MOBILITY SESSION** 15 minutes	**MOBILITY SESSION** 15 minutes	**WALK** 25 minutes	**WALK** 25 minutes	**MOBILITY SESSION** 15 minutes	**HIKE** or **WALK** in **NATURE** min. 60 minutes

down, you will still arrive at your destination. The journey will be more pleasant and enjoyable as you will feel less stressed and make fewer mistakes along the way.

Nature is a wonderful teacher. It gives us the space to connect with ourselves. Spending time outdoors in nature allows us to tune in and be present. This type of connection is crucial for optimal well-being. Whether you like to walk along the beach, sit quietly in a park or get your hands dirty in a garden, these are all beautiful opportunities for you to quiet your mind, open your heart and invite ease into your body. This type of connection is incredibly healing. Our body and our mind crave it, yet we often neglect it.

 ## YOUR WEEK 4 LIFESTYLE ASSIGNMENT

CONNECTING WITH NATURE

This week your task is to incorporate opportunities to connect with nature.

If the extent of your outside time is taking out the trash and walking to the mailbox, then you have gotten too far away from the rhythms of nature. We invite you to start reconnecting with yourself and nature today. It doesn't have to be complicated. Both of us live in a busy city and we are constantly striving to find ways to get away from the buzz to things that allow us to feel more free, grounded and alive.

Here are a few suggestions that we find helpful:

- Stop and smell the flowers during your walk.
- Notice the sounds of the birds.
- Take a barefoot walk on the beach.
- Plant some herbs or a mini garden.
- Take a moment to look up at the moon and the stars.
- Sit by a river and listen to the sound of water.
- Head out for a leisurely bike ride.
- Go hiking or camping.
- Shop at a farmers' market.
- Buy yourself flowers or a "pet" plant.
- Plan a weekend road trip to unplug from the city.
- And so on . . .

TIP: Feel free to combine this week's fitness and lifestyle assignments by going for a hike in the mountains or a forest. No matter what method of connecting with Mother Nature you choose, make sure to disconnect from distractions! If you've got your iPhone in the palm of your hand while you're hiking, you're doing it all wrong. One of the best aspects of taking a long, connected walk in nature is that it encourages you to get away from the constant social media notifications and text messages that can clog your mind and pull you even further away from your true self.

 ## WEEK 4 RESOURCES AVAILABLE FOR YOU ON WWW.ACTIVEVEGETARIAN.COM:

- Week #4 Meal Plan and Shopping List
- Meal Planning Made Simple (video)
- "How to Choose the Right Juicer" (article)
- Mobility Matters #2 (video)
- Proper Preparation for Hiking (video)
- The Healing Powers of Nature (audio)

WEEK 5

NUTRITION

"Perfection is the enemy of progress!"
—Winston Churchill

So far we have covered all the basics of a healthy plant-based weight-loss plan. But remember, *The Vegan Weight Loss Manifesto* is not a diet! When we say "diet," we're not referring to some sort of temporary and highly restrictive plan of eating in order to lose weight. If you've been searching for a solution to help you shed excess pounds and keep them off for good, you already know that diets don't work for long and often don't work at all.

I'm sure that many people can drastically reduce their calories, spend endless hours on the treadmill and give up their social life for a short period of time all in hopes to lose weight. But where is that going to get you? You will most likely ruin your metabolism, have no energy and be miserable during the entire process. Not to mention that as soon as the "diet" is over, the weight will start to creep its way back. Then what? A new diet? That's no way to live!

This eight-week plan is all about progress, NOT perfection. This week you will learn strategies for participating in social events, such as a work lunch, dinner with friends or a birthday party, while still complying with your new habits. You will learn how to make smart, healthy choices without the feeling of being deprived or left out.

YOUR WEEK 5 NUTRITION ASSIGNMENT

DINING OUT

This week's assignment is simple. Replace one of your home-prepared meals with a visit to a restaurant. Enjoy a meal out on your own or with friends, family, your boyfriend/girlfriend, your wife/husband or coworkers. Whatever you choose to eat or drink, do your best to follow nutrition habits you've been working on for the past four weeks. Also make sure to take the time to check in with yourself. Pay attention and be present. Bon appétit!

Eating out doesn't have to be unhealthy, but it does take a little more work.

Here are five tips for success:

1. Arrive prepared

Do your homework before you head out. If possible, choose a restaurant that offers vegan options. Happy Cow is a great resource to check out! Go to www.happycow.net.

For any other restaurants, see if you can view their menu online and explore your choices before you go.

2. Ask these four questions:

- How is it prepared?

Is it fried, baked, grilled, steamed...? Request to have it prepared as you like.

- Can I have the dressing on the side?

Request any dressing or sauces on the side so you can control the amount you consume.

- Can you substitute salad or veggies instead of fries?

Most places have no issue doing this, you just have to ask.

- Do you have whole grain?

Whether it is a bread basket, sandwich, pasta, etc., check and see what your options are.

3. Look at the side dishes

Often you can assemble a pretty good meal from a few side orders or appetizers, such as a baked yam, steamed edamame or a cup of fruit.

4. Keep it simple

If you feel overwhelmed or lost with the menu choices, simply order fruits and veggies. This way you have more of an understanding and control of what you are eating. Just make sure that the fruit is not served in a syrup or that the veggies are not too oily or covered in a sauce.

5. Share meals

The truth is that restaurant portions, especially in North America, are likely to be significantly larger than home-cooked meals. You're more likely to eat more at a meal in a restaurant or feel obligated to consume larger portions to get your money's worth. Why not order a meal and share it with someone?

FITNESS

"Your ability to get in shape is not based on the equipment you use. It is based on your willingness to continually and diligently work with whatever is available."

—Ross Enamait

THE IMPORTANCE OF STRENGTH TRAINING

First, we must address the question: Why should I care about strength and building muscle?

The big misconception among people who exercise to lose weight is that an endless amount of cardio is required to see results. Many shy away from any type of strength exercises as they believe that muscle will make them bulky.

Actually, the opposite is true. Having enough muscle mass is a key component for successful weight loss and overall health and fitness.

The right type of strength training is beneficial for everyone and not limited by age, gender or fitness level. Think less about how much weight you can lift and more about making your body more efficient, lean, toned and strong.

The bottom line is that no matter who you are, regular strength training will drastically improve your quality of life.

HOW BUILDING MUSCLE MAKES LIFE MORE AWESOME

Faster metabolism

With regular strength training, your metabolic rate will be higher, which basically means that the more muscle you have, the more calories you burn throughout the day. That's a huge bonus for anyone looking for long-term weight loss.

Improves your ability to do everyday activities

The stronger your muscles, the easier it is to carry your grocery bags out of the car, move some boxes around the office, push the lawnmower, play with your kids . . . the list goes on and on!

Stronger bones

Inactivity and aging can lead to a decrease in bone density, leading to brittleness. Studies have shown that consistent strength training can increase bone density and prevent, or even reverse, osteoporosis.[11]

Protects the heart

Strength training decreases blood pressure and bad cholesterol and increases good cholesterol.[12]

Fights the blues and boosts self-esteem

So often we focus on the physical health benefits of strength training, but in our experience, the mental health benefits from gaining strength are equally powerful. Strength training helps your brain release naturally occurring "feel-good" chemicals called endorphins, improving your mood and decreasing anxiety. In addition, strength training can also help increase your confidence and self-esteem.[13]

---

11   National Osteoporosis Foundation. "Fractures/Fall Prevention," last modified 2017, https://www.nof.org/patients/fracturesfall-prevention/.

12   National Strength & Conditioning Association. *Strength & Conditioning Journal.* 23(6):9-23, December 2001.

13   Stone, Michael H., Meg Stone, William A. Sands, *Principles and Practice of Resistance Training* (Champaign: Human Kinetics, 2007).

Your Body Is Your Gym

This week we will be including one strength workout in your fitness schedule. But have no fear: we are not asking you to join the world of gym rats or bodybuilder wannabes.

This workout can be done anywhere, anytime and without costly gym memberships or equipment. Bonus: It only takes about 20 minutes! The only "equipment" you will need is your own body.

Over the past two decades of my personal-training career, I came to understand just how powerful bodyweight training is. To be strong all over, you need to not only have strong muscles, but also strong joints. Because bodyweight training works the joints and tendons as they are meant to be worked, you are protecting your body from injuries.

Please don't disregard this week's fitness assignment, no matter how hard or intimidating it might seem. We have created a video for you to follow and make your first strength workout less scary. Hopefully our workout video (available online) will inspire you and motivate you to step outside your comfort zone and take that leap. Physical fitness is available to anyone who wants it. There are no secrets. Every journey starts with a single step. It's up to you to take that step and then continue the journey one day at a time. Ask yourself, how bad do I want this?

YOUR WEEK 5 FITNESS ASSIGNMENT

LET'S BUILD SOME MUSCLE

- Increase your walks to 30 minutes (or more) at least 5 times this week.
- Perform Mobility Session 3 times this week.
- Perform Strength Workout 1 time this week.
- Optional: replace one of your walks with a hike.

Your schedule can look something like this:

YOUR WEEK #5 fitness schedule*

*arrange walks, workouts and mobility sessions as needed to fit appropriately into your schedule.

MONDAY	TUESDAY	WEDNESDAY	THURSDAY	FRIDAY	SATURDAY	SUNDAY
MOBILITY SESSION 15 minutes	**WALK** 30 minutes	**STRENGTH WORKOUT** 30 minutes + **MOBILITY SESSION** 15 minutes	**WALK** 30 minutes	**WALK** 30 minutes + **MOBILITY SESSION** 15 minutes	**WALK** 30 minutes or **HIKE** in **NATURE** min. 60 minutes	**WALK** 30 minutes

LIFESTYLE

"Happiness is not something you postpone for the future; it is something you design for the present."

—Jim Rohn

When people are asked, "What do you believe is the most important thing in life?" HAPPINESS is the most popular answer.

Yet, according to a worldwide happiness survey, most North Americans and Europeans report not being overly happy.[14]

So what the heck is going on? If happiness is our primary goal in life, where are we falling short? Is it possible to be truly happy or are we striving for something out of our reach?

I used to be a chronic happiness chaser and in that race to catch it, I learned a few things. I'm sharing my personal story with you in hopes of offering an idea or approach that might help you find your life's purpose. I believe that happiness is totally achievable—it's not an easy task, but it's totally within our reach.

I'LL BE HAPPY WHEN . . .

A few years ago, I thought I had it all. I worked my butt off to get everything I believed would make me happy. I was married, had a profitable business, lived in a "dream" home, drove the "dream" car and took frequent vacations. I accomplished what I believed was the American dream and

got the approval of others, often hearing comments about how "lucky" I was and that I had "made it."

Yet inside me, there was a lot of sorrow. I wasn't laughing, I was rarely even smiling. Many times I would ask myself, "What's wrong with you?" "Why aren't you happy?" "What else do you need?"

And then one day, my dream world collapsed. In one moment, I lost it all. All those things that supposedly were making me happy were gone. Just like that! I was pretty much alone, feeling like a total failure. "What a disaster!" I thought. For a few weeks, I felt incredibly sorry for myself, which really didn't get me anywhere and only created a deeper separation and sadness in my heart. This wasn't the way I wanted to live my life! I had bigger hopes and expectations for myself. I knew there was more and I was ready to find it—this time with a different set of rules and values. I wanted to discover happiness that doesn't go away even if the things around me crumble.

Happiness Is an Inside Job

Here is something important I learned: Our desire for pleasure and happiness makes us unhappy.

Let me rephrase it. Craving happiness brings misery. Whenever you crave happiness, you invite suffering. Whenever you don't crave happiness, there it is . . . you're happy!

Ask yourself, "What is it that I'm really craving?"

We often think, "Once I have the house (car, job, partner, etc. . . .), then I'll be happy."

Really? Will you? For how long?

---

14   Sustainable Development Solutions Network. "World Happiness Report 2013," last modified 2013, http://unsdsn.org/wp-content/uploads/2014/02/WorldHappinessReport2013_online.pdf.

All of those cravings are objects of the senses—things you can see, touch, taste, hear or smell—and they all have limitations. The challenge is that our mind is not happy with limitations. Our mind craves unlimited joy and unlimited pleasure, something that our five senses cannot deliver. Trust me, it's an impossible mission. There is always going to be craving for more, bigger, better, faster, shinier . . .

Just look around you; our society is a perfect example of that chase of overconsumption yet very little satisfaction. The truth is that whenever we chase this type of fulfillment we just get disappointed, over and over again.

I am not suggesting that we need to deny ourselves all the pleasures of this modern world in order to be happy—not at all! But we need to understand that those things are just an addition to our lives, not the foundation of it.

So how do you build a solid foundation for happiness?

What Brings Me Joy

Begin by looking at your life and recognizing and becoming aware of your own personal story. What makes you happy? Where do you find fulfillment and happiness? Material things? Money? Business success? Relationships? Feelings?

Realize that happiness shouldn't be something that happens to you in the future, maybe someday, if things go well. No! Happiness is here and now, who you are now, with the people you're with, doing the things you're doing, at this moment. And if you're not with people who make you happy, doing things that make you happy . . . then you should take immediate action and change your situation.

This week you will focus on the things that bring you joy. What do you love doing most? Figure out the four to five things you love doing most in life—the things that make you happiest—and make those the foundation of your day, every day. Eliminate as much of the rest as possible.

Personally, the things that I love the most are spending time in nature, quality time with friends and family, yoga, learning about health and sharing my experience with others. I do those things daily and very little else.

Steve Jobs suggested that we ask ourselves this question every day: "If today were the last day of my life, would I want to do what I am about to do today?"

Trust me, I understand that your life circumstances might make it seem impossible to have this kind of freedom. I can assure you that if you approach things with the right attitude and dedicate yourself to the work that is required, you will be able to enjoy more freedom and live the life of your dreams . . .

YOUR WEEK 5 LIFESTYLE ASSIGNMENT

I CHOOSE HAPPINESS

Can't remember the last time you actually genuinely smiled? Sometimes life gets so fast and hectic that we almost forget to have fun and enjoy the ride. The following exercise is designed to help remind you of the things that bring you joy.

Finish each sentence with your own words. Don't spend too much time thinking, just put down the first answer that comes to mind, and don't second-guess yourself.

I feel my best when . . .

When I was a kid, I used to love . . .

I can lose track of time when I'm . . .

I feel good about myself when I'm . . .

If I had unlimited time and resources and knew I could not fail, I would choose to . . .

For a printable PDF of this exercise, go to www.activevegetarian.com.

Use the above answers to determine the four to five things you love doing most in life; the things that make you happiest. Make them the foundation of your day, every day. Eliminate as much of the rest as possible.

WEEK #5 RESOURCES AVAILABLE FOR YOU ON WWW.ACTIVEVEGETARIAN.COM:

- Week #5 Meal Plan and Shopping List
- What Plant-Based Eaters Need to Know About Losing Fat and Building Muscle (audio)
- Mobility Matters #3 (video)
- Bodyweight Strength Workout #1 (video)
- "What Brings Me Joy" exercise (printable PDF)
- Seven Secrets to Happiness (audio)

WEEK 6

NUTRITION

Welcome to your sixth week of the *Vegan Weight Loss Manifesto* plan. We hope your journey is going well and you're adapting to your new plant-based lifestyle.

This week we want to talk to you about nutritional deficiencies. This is a very important topic to address, as a vegan diet can be lacking in essential nutrients. Some individuals who choose a vegan or plant-based diet only plan their intake based on what they're eliminating, which is animal products.

When people minimize or avoid animal products, it's more difficult for them to get adequate amounts of certain dietary ingredients, including protein and other vitamins and minerals. After all, it makes perfect sense. Imagine a guy named Johnny who follows a standard American diet—burger, fries, pizza, Cheerios, meatball subs, soda, etc. This kind of diet already has a low nutritional value, is lacking in essential nutrients and is a major factor in escalating obesity rates. But that's a different story for another time.

Johnny has a sudden epiphany and decides that starting tomorrow he is done with eating meat and all other animal products—he's going to be a vegan! However, Johnny doesn't know much about nutrition or how food can affect his overall health and well-being. After all, we don't learn this fundamental knowledge at school. The only thing he knows is that meat is not part of his diet anymore. So he continues to eat fries, drink soda, orders a sub without the meatballs and in the morning munches on Cheerios straight out of the box. Once in a while he eats a few Oreo cookies because his buddy told him they are vegan.

Do you see the issue here? We cannot simply remove meat, dairy and animal fats from our life and expect miracles. In order to thrive and achieve optimal health, we must consciously get enough nutrients. This applies to everyone, vegans as well as omnivores.

At the beginning of this eight-week plan, you were given the task to remove all the junk food from your house and replace it with healthy, plant-based foods. There was a very good reason for that assignment.

Whole, fresh foods are packed with nutrients and basing your diet around them will provide your body with proper nourishment and satisfy most of your nutritional needs.

You probably noticed we used the word "most". Let us explain. We are big believers that nature provides us with an abundance of everything we need for optimal health. However, we humans tend to mess with Mother Nature.

Our food (even organic) no longer has the same nutritional value it had 100 or even 50 years ago. Our soil is lacking in minerals; farmers spray their crops; food travels to us from different countries or even continents. Additionally, toxins exist in the environment. These are among the reasons that it's really hard to get all the essential vitamins and minerals from food alone.

DO I NEED TO TAKE SUPPLEMENTS?[15]

Depending on your lifestyle, many of you will find it necessary to supplement your whole-food vegan diet with protein, B vitamins (especially B_{12}), vitamin D, essential fatty acids and minerals such as zinc.

Let's take a closer look at each of them:

Protein

A quality protein powder isn't mandatory, but can be useful to ensure optimal protein intake. We prefer to use RAW Organic Protein Powder by Garden of Life. It works really well in our morning smoothies, protein bars and even homemade "ice creams."

You can find some of our recipes that include protein powder Five-Ingredient Protein Bars (page 142), Active Recovery (page 68) and Very Berry Blast Nicecream (page 153).

Best plant-based sources: beans and legumes, nuts, seeds, dark leafy greens and high-protein whole grains such as quinoa.

Deficiency signs: trouble building muscle mass, low energy levels and fatigue, poor concentration and trouble learning, moodiness and mood swings, muscle, bone and joint pain, thinning hair and brittle nails, low immunity and slow-healing wounds.

---

15   The Vegan Society. "How to thrive on a plant-based diet," last modified 2017, https://www.vegansociety.com/resources/nutrition-and-health/overview.

B Vitamins (especially B$_{12}$)

B vitamins are definitely important for energy, hormone optimization and overall health. They get depleted when we are under stress. Very low B$_{12}$ intake can cause anemia and nervous system damage.

Best plant-based sources: B$_{12}$ is often found in nutritional yeast, miso and chlorella.

Deficiency signs: memory problems, disorientation or dementia, fatigue, tingling in the hands and feet, sore mouth and tongue.[16]

Other B vitamin deficiency signs include red or difficult-to-control eyes, cracked lips, skin rashes and digestive issues.

Vitamin D

Everyone needs vitamin D. Depending on the season (our bodies can't make enough vitamin D from half an hour in the sun in winter months due to the angle of the sun), you can spend half an hour outside each day or take a supplement. Vitamin D is essential for strong bones as it helps the body use calcium from the diet.

Best plant-based sources: Sunlight is the best source.

Supplements: D$_2$ is animal-free and D$_3$ is often animal-derived.

Deficiency signs: Bone pain and muscle weakness, sadness and high blood pressure.

Essential Fatty Acids

Our bodies need two specific fatty acids from our diet—omega-3 and omega-6—and the rest can be produced in our body from eating enough healthy fats (avocados, soaked nuts and seeds, olives, etc.). Essential fatty acids assist in the development and function of the brain and nervous system and they help regulate proper thyroid and adrenal activity. They play a role in thinning your blood, which can prevent blood clots that can lead to heart attacks and strokes. They also possess natural anti-inflammatory qualities that can relieve symptoms of both arthritis and other autoimmune system diseases.

Best plant-based sources: flax, hemp, walnuts, green leafy vegetables and algae supplements.

Deficiency signs: mood swings, memory loss, dementia, vision problems, hair and skin problems and menstrual cramps.

Zinc

Zinc is a powerful mineral that's needed for a healthy immune system. It also helps your hormones, thyroid and blood sugar function properly. It assists in the breakdown of carbohydrates for energy, which is very important for a healthy metabolism, and it also assists with testosterone and insulin function in the body.

Best plant-based sources: pumpkin seeds, spinach, beans and chickpeas.

Deficiency signs: frequent colds, leaky gut, consistent diarrhea, poor vision, infertility, thinning hair, stunted growth in children and slow-healing wounds.

Digestive Enzymes

If you have difficulties digesting food, suffer with bloating and gas or food allergies, you might benefit from taking digestive enzymes. And speaking of digestive issues . . .

Probiotics

Most people, including children, are in need of a probiotic boost once in a while. This is due to multiple factors, including the use of prescription medication—particularly antibiotics—in addition to high-carbohydrate diets, the consumption of chlorinated and fluoridated water, and conventional foods such as non-organic meat and dairy that contain antibiotic residues. These chemicals kill off probiotics in your system, and over time, they can damage your digestive track. We personally find probiotics very helpful with keeping our immune systems strong. We prefer RAW Probiotic by Garden of Life. These probiotics are never heated to more than 115°F (46°C)—this process maintains more live nutrients, enzymes and probiotic strains.

There are a few other important nutrients to pay attention to:

Calcium: from leafy green vegetables, raw sesame seeds, tahini and soaked almonds

Iron: from beans, spinach, pumpkin seeds and spirulina

Magnesium: from dark leafy vegetables, avocados, bananas, figs, soaked nuts and seeds

Iodine: from seaweed and dulse

---

16   Iris, July 5, 2010 (12:55 a.m.), re: What are classic B12 Deficiency Symptoms?, "Raw," vegsource.com, http://www.vegsource.com/talk/raw/messages/100021261.html.

WHAT IF I AM CONCERNED ABOUT MISSING SOMETHING?

Take notes and make an appointment with your healthcare provider. Your needs might be different from ours, so don't assume that because certain supplements work for us, you need to take the same. We get a full bloodwork analysis done on a yearly basis so we know exactly what our bodies need and only supplement those missing nutrients.

YOUR WEEK 6 NUTRITION ASSIGNMENT

AM I MISSING SOMETHING?

This week your assignment is to schedule a complete blood profile test, performed by a reputable doctor you trust.

Getting annual bloodwork with a physician or a health expert is a very important part of your health and overall well-being. We always stress to our clients the importance of prevention. Don't wait until something is wrong. Be proactive and take full responsibility for your own health. With regular blood tests, you will be able to observe trends and catch potential health problems before they spiral out of control.

Ask your health care provider to carefully explain all the results to you. If they say that everything is normal, request a copy of the lab report and ask for a second opinion.

The results from your bloodwork can also be very beneficial for your weight-loss success. Missing certain nutrients can easily affect your energy and metabolism and cause cravings.

If you want to track your results over time, make sure to request a copy of your lab report and keep it filed in a safe place.

For more about nutritional deficiencies, listen to a podcast series on the topic at www.activevegetarian.com.

FITNESS

> "The body is your temple. Keep it pure and clean for the soul to reside in."
>
> —B.K.S. Iyengar

Namaste. For the first decade of my fitness career, I didn't pay any attention to yoga. I put most of my emphasis on high-intensity workouts, lifting weights and getting a good sweat on, because those were the things I knew would deliver results. Yoga wasn't even on my radar, mostly because I didn't think it could "compete" with any of the

previously mentioned strategies as far as weight loss and overall physical health goes. Boy, was I wrong!

I finally surrendered to the world of yoga about five years ago, and it has hugely shifted my perception on health, fitness and life in general. So much so that Nikki and I now make an annual trip to India—the motherland of yoga—to further explore the teachings and deepen our practice. These continued studies have helped us to understand the transformative power and the real value of yoga. We believe that the benefits are so vast that this eight-week plan wouldn't be complete without it.

There are many misconceptions about yoga. Some people believe that yoga is only for those who are already physically fit, while others (like the old me) don't see much value in it. If you have never given yoga an honest chance, this week is your time. I encourage you to read and complete this week's assignment so you can experience the transformational benefits of yoga for yourself. It doesn't matter what your current state of health or life circumstances may be—just do it.

THE AMAZING BENEFITS OF YOGA

Rather than listing all of the scientifically supported health benefits of yoga,[17] I feel it would be much more powerful to hear from real people and their experience with yoga.

What benefits have you experienced since starting yoga?

"I experience less physical pain and I feel that my body appreciates me back."

"What benefits haven't I experienced? The physical benefits alone have been worth it—weight loss, flexibility, more energy. But it also made me curious about changing the rest of my life. Specifically, my diet and my mental/emotional state. So much healthier and calmer now!"

"My life is so incredibly rich and purposeful. I have a reason to get out of bed each day."

"When you have felt the magnificence of your body in a vinyasa class or a slow flow class, then you know that you're making a bad choice when you eat 10 pieces of fried chicken or half a pizza. You don't want to abuse your body when you know how good it can feel."

---

17   Kirkwood, G, Rampes H, Tuffrey V, et al "Yoga for anxiety: a systematic review of the research evidence," *British Journal of Sports Medicine* (2005), doi: 39:884-891.

"I have experienced a natural rise in my energy levels. I am less tempted to snack on junk food throughout the day because I don't feel the need to have a sugary pick-me-up to beat the after-lunch blues."

"For me, that resulted in better posture and less tension in my lower back."

"It's so rare that anyone gets a decent night's sleep nowadays and I feel like yoga significantly contributes to the best sleep I've ever gotten in my life."

"One of the most surprising things I saw as a result of my first yoga session is that I was a lot less stressed out leaving than I was going in."

"I find that I am now more focused on my goals and intentions."

"I swear it reduces chronic pain. I don't know how, I don't know why, but it works better than drugs."

Many people improve their lives through regular yoga practice, not only on the physical level but also on mental and spiritual levels.

Even if yoga plays only a small role in your life, it can make meaningful contributions to all your health and fitness goals. But here is the key—you must take the first step!

YOUR WEEK 6 FITNESS ASSIGNMENT

MY YOGA

This week your assignment is to create time in your schedule for one (or more) yoga practices.

You can either join Nikki and follow her gentle yoga session on our website or find a reputable yoga studio in your city and sign up for a class.

Keep in mind that yoga comes in many forms and is taught in many ways; therefore, finding the right yoga for you is important. So do try a few different styles to find the right one for you. Don't stress if you can't touch your toes; that's why we call it yoga "practice".

- Continue your regular 30-minute (or more) walks at least 5 times this week.
- Perform Mobility Session 3 times this week.
- Perform Strength Workout 1 time this week.
- Include Yoga 1 time this week.
- Optional: replace one of your walks with a hike.

Your schedule can look something like this:

YOUR WEEK #6 fitness schedule*

*arrange walks, workouts and mobility/yoga sessions as needed to fit appropriately into your schedule.

MONDAY	TUESDAY	WEDNESDAY	THURSDAY	FRIDAY	SATURDAY	SUNDAY
STRENGTH WORKOUT 30 minutes + **MOBILITY SESSION** 15 minutes	**WALK** 30 minutes	**WALK** 30 minutes + **MOBILITY SESSION** 15 minutes	**WALK** 30 minutes	**WALK** 30 minutes + **MOBILITY SESSION** 15 minutes	**YOGA SESSION**	**WALK** or **HIKE** in **NATURE** min. 60 minutes

LIFESTYLE

"Stress is like spice—in the right proportion it enhances the flavor of a dish. Too little produces a bland, dull meal; too much may choke you."

—Donald Tubesing

Have you ever thought about what role stress plays in your efforts to lose weight?

We read about it all the time—stress is making us sick and creates imbalances—yet many of us do not entirely understand why or how this happens or what to do about it.

The truth is that you can eat the "perfect" diet and you can exercise every single day, but if you are not managing your stress levels correctly, your efforts will be sabotaged.

It's important to understand that stress is a natural part of our lives. It's pretty much impossible to avoid as it is a normal physiological response to events that make you feel threatened or upset. Many of us will even find healthy amounts of stress to be a beneficial thing—keeping us focused, alert and at the top of our game.

Too much stress, or the wrong kind of stress, is the largest cause of health problems in many people's lives. This "bad" stress is often referred to as chronic stress; it builds up slowly over time. What happens is this: stress hormones (adrenaline and cortisol) are released, over and over again, in non-threatening situations or by a series of inappropriate triggers such as:

- Work deadlines
- Challenging coworkers or bosses
- Anxiety about money
- Being overwhelmed by having too much to do
- Poor communication with your spouse or partner
- Not having enough time for family or personal life
- Being stuck in traffic/running late

When your autonomic nervous system is activated continuously or repeatedly by "false alarms," it forgets how and when to turn itself off. A body overloaded with adrenaline and cortisol is a body suffering from chronic stress. [18]

---

18   Carnegie Mellon University. "How stress influences disease: Study reveals inflammation as the culprit," Science Daily. ScienceDaily, last modified April 2, 2012, https://www.sciencedaily.com/releases/2012/04/120402162546.htm.

YOUR WEEK 6 LIFESTYLE ASSIGNMENT

STRESS MANAGEMENT

This week we invite you to find healthy methods to manage stressful situations. We say "healthy methods" because often people cope with stress in harmful ways—alcohol, smoking, drugs, bingeing on food, undereating, snapping at people, watching TV, procrastinating and more. This approach only makes matters worse and often leads to anxiety and depression.

We believe that everyone should learn and practice ways to cope with stress. Just imagine the difference it would make—what would your work performance look like? What about the interactions with colleagues, friends and people you love?

This assignment has two parts. In the first part, you will identify the ways that you believe would help you relieve the accumulated stress you might be feeling. In the second portion of this task, we ask you to consider a few strategies that would help prevent or at least minimize the stress in your life.

WAYS TO RELIEVE STRESS:

- One-Minute Meditation (page 34)
- Spend more time in nature
- Exercise and yoga
- Take a bath with Epsom salts
- Avoid stress-promoting foods (coffee, energy drinks, sodas, alcohol and fried and processed foods)
- Eat "grounding" foods (carrots, sweet potatoes, root vegetables, berries, figs, melons, yams, mango and avocado)
- Take a brief walk
- Take 10 deep breaths
- Get some sunshine
- Listen to relaxing music
- Drink herbal or green tea
- Unplug from the digital world
- Get a massage

WAYS TO HELP PREVENT AND MINIMIZE STRESS

Simplify and Organize

Take time to get things in your life organized, starting with your desk and any clutter in your environment. Clean out, tidy up and minimize your home, closets and car.

Time Management

Lack of time is often a major stress factor for many people. There are several effective ways to manage your time wisely and avoid feeling under pressure—create a daily plan, block out distractions, track your time, prioritize, delegate, etc.

Sleep Is Crucial

Staying up late to get more done robs you of your total productivity. It dulls your mind, increases stress, promotes weight gain and contributes to mood swings. Get your eight hours, no matter what. Take a nap if you missed your sleep. Prioritize sleep.

Be Present and in the Moment

Instead of rushing through life, learn to take things slow. Enjoy your food, enjoy the people around you and enjoy nature. This approach alone can save tons of stress.

Evaluate Your Commitments and Learn to Say "NO"

We all have many commitments in our life—work, kids, spouse, things to do at home, social obligations, spiritual commitments, hobbies and more. Consider each of them and remove the ones that stress you out the most.

Exercise and Eat Healthy

Exercising helps relieve built-up stress, and your daily walks and mobility sessions give you some quiet time to contemplate and relax, all while you are getting more fit. A fitter person is better equipped to handle stress. What you eat also plays an important role. A healthy diet can help counter the impact of stress by strengthening the immune system and lowering blood pressure.

Express Gratitude

Seriously! Learn to be grateful for what you have and for the people in your life and see them as a gift. If you practice this outlook on life, you will reduce stress and happiness will grow.

Have Fun

Do something you enjoy each day, even if it's just for a few minutes. Play a game with your kids, find an activity or a hobby you enjoy, refer back to the What Brings Me Joy exercise (page 42) . . . Whatever you choose—be sure to laugh.

Stress is just another bad habit we pick up as we go through life. The beautiful thing is that if this habit doesn't serve us, we have the choice to give it up or replace it with something constructive that will allow us to grow and thrive.

For more tips and ideas on how to manage stress in a healthy way, go to www.activevegetarian.com.

WEEK 6 RESOURCES AVAILABLE FOR YOU ON WWW.ACTIVEVEGETARIAN.COM:

- Week #6 Meal Plan and Shopping List
- "Nutritional Deficiencies" podcast series (audio)
- Mobility Matters #4 (video)
- Bodyweight Strength Workout #2 (video)
- My Yoga #1 (video)
- "How to Manage Stress in a Healthy Way" (audio)

WEEK 7

NUTRITION

"Eat real food, not too much. Mostly plants."
—Michael Pollan

WHAT EXACTLY IS "REAL FOOD"?

Real food is wholesome and nourishing. It is simple, unprocessed (or minimally processed), whole food. Real food is pure and as close to its natural form as possible. Real food is the best way to heal your body of disease. Real food is the key to optimal health.

Does it mean that you have to eat everything raw?

No.

The word "processed" can often be confusing. Unless you adopt a fully raw diet, you will eat foods that have been processed in some way. Apples are cut from trees, quinoa is cooked, olive oil is pressed.

But there is a difference between mechanical processing and chemical processing.

If it's a single-ingredient food with no added chemicals, then it's perfectly fine if it's been ground or put into a jar. It's still real food.

However, at each stage of the food-preparation process, nutrients and flavor are lost, and chemicals, preservatives and flavor-enhancers, like salt and sugar, are added. That's why it's important to eat food that is as close to its natural state as possible.

Here are a few examples for you:

- Steel-cut oats versus instant oats with maple sugar flavor
- Natural peanut butter versus peanut butter with hydrogenated oils and sugar
- Fresh tomatoes versus store-bought ketchup
- Homemade mashed potatoes versus instant boxed potatoes
- Olive oil and vinegar versus store-bought salad dressing

The more processed the food is, the lower the nutritional value of the food. Unfortunately, the majority of the foods available in an average supermarket are highly processed.

This is a problem, as it directly relates to the state of our health. Any time you consume processed foods—such as breakfast cereals, chips, bagels, hot dogs, sodas and other man-made packaged food—you create inflammation in your body. When inflammation is out of control, it can seriously damage the body and become the source of most chronic illnesses. Inflammation has long been known to play a role in allergic diseases like asthma, arthritis and Crohn's disease, but recently many studies have shown that Alzheimer's

disease, cancer, cardiovascular disease, diabetes, high blood pressure, high cholesterol levels and Parkinson's disease may all be related to chronic inflammation in the body.[19] [20] Not to mention that when the body experiences so much stress, achieving a healthy weight is pretty much an impossible task.

YOUR WEEK 7 NUTRITION ASSIGNMENT

THE FIVE-INGREDIENT CHALLENGE

From now on, any time you go grocery shopping, stick to the Five-Ingredient Rule:

- If the product in your hands has more than five ingredients, put it back on the shelf.
- If one of the five ingredients is something you've never heard of or you can't pronounce it, put it back on the shelf.
- If you have no idea about how this product is made (i.e., you couldn't make it at home with ingredients in your kitchen), then your body probably doesn't know how to process it either; put it back on the shelf.

Those five ingredients also have to be free from:

- Hydrogenated/partially hydrogenated oils
- High-fructose corn syrup
- Added sugars (including hidden sources like syrups)
- Artificial colors (e.g., FD&C Blue #1)
- Animal ingredients

---

19   European Society of Cardiology. *European Heart Journal.* 27(6):15-20, August 2006.

20   Monteiro, Rosário and Isabel Azevedo. "Chronic Inflammation in Obesity and the Metabolic Syndrome," Mediators of Inflammation (2010), doi: 10.1155/2010/289645.

WHAT IF A RECIPE HAS MORE THAN FIVE INGREDIENTS?

A long list of real food ingredients in a recipe is not the same thing. As long as all listed ingredients are wholesome and real food, it's all good!

FITNESS

"It's not the daily increase but daily decrease. Hack away at the unessential."

—Bruce Lee

One of the most common complaints we hear from clients is "I don't have time to work out." We get it—most of us live busy lives, juggling responsibilities and tasks, trying to fit more things into our already over-scheduled days. Among all of the buzz, finding time for daily exercise might seem almost impossible.

We have some good news, though. There is a solution for all you busybodies out there. It's called interval training.

Interval training is a way of moving the body in which you alternate periods of high-intensity exercise with low-intensity recovery periods. For instance, during walking, if you're in decent shape, you might incorporate short bursts of jogging into your regular brisk walks. If you're less fit, you might alternate leisurely walking with periods of faster walking. You can also implement this principle with your strength workouts by performing squats for, say, 20 seconds for as many proper repetitions as possible followed by a 10-second rest. Then repeat this cycle several times.

This style of exercise is not only time efficient but it also provides numerous health benefits. Let's look at some of the perks of interval training; notice that many of them closely correlate with weight loss:[21]

You Burn More Calories

The more vigorously you exercise, the more calories you'll burn—even if you increase intensity for just a few minutes at a time.

---

21   Trapp, E G, D J Chisholm, J Freund and S H Boutcher "The effects of high-intensity intermittent exercise training on fat loss and fasting insulin levels of young women," *International Journal of Obesity* (2008), doi: 10.1038/sj.ijo.0803781.

Good Health from the Inside Out

As your cardiovascular fitness improves, you'll be able to exercise longer or with more intensity. Imagine finishing your 30-minute walk in 20 minutes—or the additional calories you'll burn by keeping up the pace for the full half hour. This is fantastic news for your heart! Other amazing bodily changes you'll experience include firmer skin, fewer wrinkles, increased energy, boosted metabolism, improved libido, improved muscle tone, reduced body fat and greater "mental toughness."

No Special Equipment Needed

You can simply modify your current routine. If you're walking outdoors, try walking faster between certain mailboxes, trees or other landmarks.

There Is a Catch

In order to experience these benefits, you have to be willing to put in your maximal effort during the high-intensity periods and get out of your comfort zone.

Can Anyone Do Interval Training?

Interval training isn't appropriate for everyone. If you have a chronic health condition or haven't been exercising regularly, consult your doctor before trying any type of interval training.

INTERVAL training**WORKOUT**

ACTIVITY	TIME	INTENSITY (1–10)
Warm up	5 minutes	3.5
Walk briskly	1 minute	6
Walk at moderate pace	2 minutes	5
Walk as fast as possible	1 minute	8
Walk slowly	2 minutes	4
Walk as fast as possible	1 minute	8
Walk at moderate pace	2 minutes	5
Walk briskly	1 minute	6
Cool down	5 minutes	3.5

Recent studies suggest, however, that interval training can be used safely for short periods even in individuals with heart disease,[22] as long as your doc gives the okay.

Also, keep the risk of overuse injury in mind. Your body needs time to heal itself after this kind of training. We recommend that you do no more than three interval training sessions per week.

Are you ready to give this a try?

YOUR WEEK 7 FITNESS ASSIGNMENT

INTERVAL TRAINING TIME

This week you will challenge yourself with one interval training session. For this assignment, you can choose from one of the three options:

Option 1: Replace one of your regular walks with an interval walk.

Option 2: Join us for an Interval Training Time (ITT) workout on our site.

Option 3: For extra bonus points, do both options 1 and 2.

---

22   Shiraev, Tim and Gabriella Barclay, "Clinical benefits of high intensity interval training," Australian Family Physician 41 (2012): 960-962.

Your schedule can look something like this:

- Continue your regular 30-minute (or more) walks at least 4 times this week.
- Perform Mobility Session 3 times this week.
- Perform Strength Workout 1 time this week.
- Include Yoga Practice 1 time this week.
- Include an Interval Walk or Interval Training Time.
- Optional: Replace one of your walks with a hike.

LIFESTYLE

"You can't force others to change. The best you can hope for is to inspire them with your actions."
—Zuzana Fajkusova

By now, we're sure you've already encountered individuals who were less than supportive and made you really test your commitment to your new lifestyle. Sometimes it might be your friends, and other times it's your family or coworkers who believe that they're doing you a favor. They tell you to "relax, you're taking this too seriously," or "come on, just this one time won't hurt you."

YOUR WEEK #7 fitness schedule*

*arrange walks, workouts and mobility/yoga sessions as needed to fit appropriately into your schedule.

MONDAY	TUESDAY	WEDNESDAY	THURSDAY	FRIDAY	SATURDAY	SUNDAY
INTERVAL WORKOUT 20 minutes + **MOBILITY SESSION** 15 minutes	**WALK** 30 minutes	**STRENGTH WORKOUT** 30 minutes + **MOBILITY SESSION** 15 minutes	**WALK** 30 minutes	**WALK** 30 minutes + **MOBILITY SESSION** 15 minutes	**YOGA SESSION**	**HIKE** or **WALK** in **NATURE** min. 60 minutes

I have been on this plant-based lifestyle journey for the past 20 years and the majority of my friends and family members understand that this is ME—not a phase, not a health kick, not a crash diet or crazy hippie moment of mine: That for me, it's my LIFE. For those of you who have recently had the epiphany to transform your health and take control of your life, situations like the ones mentioned can negatively impact your journey. They may even make you give up altogether.

We all want the people in our lives to cheer us on and support us. Perhaps they could even join us on our quest to better health. Rightfully so, after all, we all want our loved ones to enjoy good health and be happy, right? So why is it that when we finally make that decision to change, we encounter resistance from those same people?

In order to help us understand the reasoning behind this behavior, we need to dig into human psychology for a moment.

Humans are social creatures. We want to fit in. We thrive in groups. We learn from and inspire each other. Due to these instinctual social tendencies, we live by a tribal mindset.

Naturally, we don't want to feel left out from our "tribe," no matter how broken the social standards might be. We fear the consequences that could arise from stepping out of line and challenging some of those made-up social norms. This is exactly why we have a hard time succeeding at being different and standing up for what we feel is right. The brave ones who do are often rejected and picked on, at least at the beginning.

Did you know that in some cultures around the world, it is considered a sin or a shameful betrayal to challenge social or cultural norms, even if they go against your ethics or human rights?

Fortunately, changing your eating and exercise habits is perfectly legal, so let's see how you can safely handle any negative or demotivating outside influences.

BECOME A PEACEFUL WARRIOR

We live in a world where being unhealthy and sedentary, "dining" at fast-food restaurants, depending on medication, smoking and drinking are more acceptable than the opposite. It's not easy to step out of the "tribe" and be different, but if you are serious about your health, it's an absolute MUST.

It's not as much of a lonely journey as it might seem. This is a very exciting time for anyone interested in vegan living! The growth of plant-based diets and lifestyles over the past few years has been tremendous. We are seeing countless best-selling books, award-winning documentaries and more vegan-promoting festivals and events than ever before. And we cannot ignore the growing number of celebrities, professional athletes and influential people adopting and endorsing a vegan lifestyle.

This is a perfect time for you to become a peaceful warrior—break away from social norms that no longer serve you and claim back your personal power. No more masks, no more trying to fit in—enough playing small and settling for less than you deserve. If you are truly serious about your health, it's time to stand up for yourself. Dare to give up living your life to other people's expectations and start living it your way instead. The road won't always be easy, but it will be worth it.

YOUR WEEK 7 LIFESTYLE ASSIGNMENT

THE ART OF BEING HEALTHY IN AN UNHEALTHY WORLD

This week, we want to offer suggestions and strategies to help you navigate through four types of social pressure that you might encounter while embracing a plant-based diet and healthy lifestyle.

COWORKERS

Most of us spend a large amount of time around coworkers—around 50 percent of total waking hours during any given working day, to be exact!

Sometimes an office environment can feel very much like high school all over again—complete with cliques, secrets, gossip and drama. It's no wonder we may feel under peer pressure to fit in. When Bob has the "brilliant" idea to pick up three dozen doughnuts on the way to work, we're sure he doesn't want to be caught eating them all by himself . . . So he wanders around the office, trying to find other people to help him power through. Once he makes his way over to your desk and you politely decline, you know you'll hear something along the lines of, "Oh come on! It's just one doughnut!"

But Bob is not the only one who can provide you with a challenge. We've heard stories from clients whose coworkers poked fun at them for bringing their own salad and power smoothie for lunch.

So what's the solution? First, there is a chance that your dietary choices will be the source of jokes and mockery from your coworkers.

Why? If your coworkers are unhealthy and uninterested in making smarter diet choices, then the thought of someone in their office making positive life changes, exercising and adjusting their diet might make them feel inadequate. After all, plant-based eating requires self-control and discipline. For most of them, it's painful to watch you succeed, as it stirs up a lot of their own insecurities. It's much easier to drag you down with them than deal with their own issues.

We wish we could give you a magic spell that would turn all the Debbie Downers into your biggest supporters, but unfortunately we can't.

So here's the deal . . . it's time to suck it up!

Practice being a peaceful warrior. Stay calm and collected. Be strong and know your determination will pay off in the long run. For the first few weeks, you might get funny looks when you bring in your own meals. Someone may make fun of you.

However, as you start to transform, the "What's that, swamp water you're drinking?" comments will start to switch to "Wow, you look good! Where do you get all this energy from?" Then, "How did you do it?" and eventually, "Can you help me?"

The beginning can be rough . . . Be proud to stand out and be different! Be the leader!

FAMILY

The old saying goes, "You can pick your friends, but you can't pick your family."

What we learn is what we do.

To be more specific, the habits we learn from our parents or guardians can be extremely difficult to break. Our brains are more impressionable during our early years and therefore the things we learn often become deeply ingrained.

My grandmother was an exceptional cook and she often expressed her love through food. She would make a huge spread even if there was just one extra person at her house.

Growing up, I had a strong connection with my grandma and some of my best memories are of helping her in the kitchen. I believe that my passion for cooking came from her. In my early teens, when I decided to give up meat, she had a very difficult time accepting my choice. Today I understand why—she received love from me by pleasing me with the food she prepared. When I no longer wanted the food, she felt like the love was being rejected. Unfortunately, it put quite a strain on our relationship.

Are you experiencing a similar scenario? Perhaps you grew up in a family where the only activity you did as a kid was walk to and from school and now you find it very difficult to commit to exercise. Perhaps you watched your father overeat and now you have an unhealthy relationship with food yourself. Whatever the situation might be, don't lose hope.

Maybe you can't control the actions of your parents, grandparents or siblings, but you can control your own. Here are several things you can try that may help.

Rather than thinking, "No one in my family is healthy; no one understands the importance of clean eating and exercise; I'm all alone," think about the opportunity you have right in front of you. You could help change your own family's health and mindset and even those of future generations. It starts with you. A big responsibility, but kind of cool, huh?

Here are a few things to consider. Don't try to force others to change, and don't get frustrated or upset, as that will only backfire. Instead, stand strong with your choices and set an inspiring example for others to follow. Be strong in your convictions and offer suggestions, like, "Hey, Mom, can I cook dinner for the family tonight? It's going to be a healthier version of lasagna. I'm really excited about it."

One last thing to keep in mind—patience and gentleness is power. Allow your loved ones the time to adjust to your new way of living, and be kind and supportive. Perhaps at the beginning there may be a lot of resistance from them, but after your transformation, you might start to get a few questions like, "Our doctor told your dad that he needs to drop a few pounds—any tips?"

You can't force others to change. The best you can hope for is to inspire them with your actions.

FRIENDS

Our friends have a big influence over the way we think, feel and behave. As it happens, friends who commonly conspire together also enjoy indulgences together. That's why it's important to think carefully about the people you spend your free time with.

Clients often comment on their struggle with their social lives and the negative impact it has on their health. Spending time with old friends generally involves going out to eat, drink and engage in activities that no longer support your new healthy habits. Your friends might have a hard time understanding your sudden change and probably have absolutely no interest in embracing your new ways.

We get it; it's not easy. These are your friends, the people you hang out with after work and on weekends! They might be lazy and unmotivated . . . but does it mean you have to ditch them?

One thing you should know beforehand is that it's going to be way easier for them to drag you back down to their lifestyle choices rather than watch you take off on your own. The old saying "misery loves company" is pretty accurate here—overweight, out-of-shape, unmotivated people don't want to feel alone. So if you have friends like this and you choose to spend time with them, you have to be strong and okay with being different.

Here are some other suggestions:

Get Them Excited

Definitely not an easy task, but it can be done. Explain what you are doing and why. Ask for their support. You never know; they might be feeling the same way as you are and ready for a fresh start.

Be the Black Sheep

Get over those sarcastic comments and their cheap jokes and continue moving forward, doing your own thing. Sure, you will still have to deal with them making fun of you bringing kale chips to a party or going for a walk before you meet up on a Friday night, but who cares! That's what friends do, no? As Kanye West says, "that that don't kill me can only make me stronger." You can thank them later.

Find Some New Friends

If you really care about your old friends, don't abandon them. Simply open yourself up to new connections. It is said that we are an average of the five people we associate with most. Perhaps find friends that inspire you and motivate you to be a better you—People you can learn from and grow closer to with your desired goals in mind.

YOUR PARTNER

This is probably going to be the toughest one out of all of them. You might be so ready to change your lifestyle and your eating habits and get your body back, but there is one big challenge . . .

Often, the person you are in an intimate relationship with has either no desire to consider healthy changes and/or they don't want you to change your ways.

Well . . . this really sucks.

Don't give up. Not yet. We have a couple of ways you can try to make this work.

Just like with your friends, sit your partner down and explain to them your whys. Do your best to describe what this change means to you and how strongly you want it. Then allow them to have their own opinion. Pay attention to what they have to say and perhaps you might find that they are also ready to make a change for the better. If that's the case, awesome! Encourage your partner and offer support.

If they don't feel the same excitement toward a healthy lifestyle that you do, don't get upset. Accept their opinion without judgment and resentment, and understand we are all individuals and need to find our own path.

You can gently show them ways to lead a healthier lifestyle by finding an activity that you two enjoy together. Hiking, walking the dog, Frisbee, yoga, dancing, whatever! The key is that you both enjoy it and do it on a regular basis.

There's a strong possibility that once you start doing more activities together, you both will start to feel and think healthier. You never know, maybe your partner will be more open to exploring your enthusiasm for this healthy approach to life.

Do you enjoy eating meals together? Perfect! Offer to cook. A healthy, romantic dinner by candlelight is totally going to score you major brownie points.

Ask for what you need. Often friction in a relationship is caused by a lack of communication. Your partner's support may be important to you, but did you tell them how much it means to you? Did you explain to them that you want to live a better life and that having them on your side means the world to you?

We can tell you from experience that sharing your life with someone who doesn't have the same healthy, ethical or moral values as you do is difficult, but it doesn't have to be a deal breaker. You can use it as an opportunity to be the leading example. Do it without expectations. Be patient and gentle, as a change this big could take some time.

We hope the preceding examples gave you some ideas on how to handle your reactions next time someone challenges your decisions. Stay strong and we bet that your positive changes, healthy habits and improved outlook on life will have a beneficial effect on your partner, friend, parents or coworkers. Remember to stay cool, without judging or displaying any anger about their choices. Just be your awesome self, because that is the best way to inspire someone toward change.

WEEK 7 RESOURCES AVAILABLE FOR YOU ON WWW.ACTIVEVEGETARIAN.COM:

- Week #7 Meal Plan and Shopping List
- Mobility Session #5 (video)
- Bodyweight Strength Workout #3 (video)
- My Yoga #2 (video)
- Interval Training Time #1 (video)
- How to Deal with Social Pressure (audio)
- "I Can't Believe It's Vegan!" (article + recipes)

WEEK 8

You are truly awesome! You have made it to the final week of this transformation plan. We are so proud of you and hope that while reading these words, you are feeling healthy, good about yourself and happy with how far you have come.

This final week of our program is exciting—well, at least to us as coaches. This is where all your efforts come together and form a solid foundation for a healthy body and happy life. So let's dive in!

NUTRITION

> "Success is the sum of small efforts, repeated day in and day out."
>
> —Robert Collier

Food—friend or foe? It can either be our best ally or our worst enemy. It's a choice you have to make. Food can provide nourishment and reward you with a healthy body or it can lead to physical pain and emotional suffering.

Anyone who has ever attempted to lose weight understands how challenging this balancing act can be. For most of us,

food is easily accessible and readily available pretty much anywhere and at any time of the day. We talk about food, we share food, we prepare food, we watch TV shows dedicated to food . . . we are surrounded by it. I honestly believe that food has become the drug of our century. It no longer serves as a means of nourishment; instead we use food to mask pain, to express happiness, to hide sadness . . .

But let's be honest—food doesn't solve these issues. It doesn't change our sadness, take away our loneliness or kill our boredom. At least not in the long term. Sooner or later, that feeling will return and leave you craving more. Now you have a "hangry" monster on your hands—the true enemy.

Those of you who diligently followed along with this book, adopted the prescribed healthy habits and completed your weekly assignments don't have to fear food anymore. You are on a solid path that will help you stay on track, take charge and free yourself from the dieting roller coaster. Remember that what you eat and how much goes way beyond weight loss. Having a solid healthy relationship with food is the catalyst for true transformation.

WHAT IF I DIDN'T STICK TO THE EIGHT-WEEK PLAN?

Did you get lost or distracted for a moment, but deep down you know you are ready for a change? Don't give up! We suggest you go back to Week 1 (page 16) and take another shot at it—this time, with the intention of giving it 100 percent!

YOUR WEEK 8 NUTRITION ASSIGNMENT

CONSISTENCY IS KEY

The key to long-term success is to stay consistent with your diet-related habits:

- Keep your kitchen free of junk food.
- Drink at least 8 cups (2 L) of fresh water daily.
- Consume only real, whole, plant-based foods and avoid all processed foods.
- Cook or prepare the majority of your own meals.
- Don't deprive yourself: eat five balanced meals spread out through the day.
- Perform the One-Minute Meditation (page 34) on a regular basis or any time you feel the temptation to break any of the preceding habits.

EXERCISE

"Nothing happens until you move."

—*Robin Sharma*

It's quite obvious that in order to drop unwanted weight and get healthy, you need to move. When exercise is combined with good nutritional habits, the results can be amazing. We've seen this many times before with coaching our clients as well as in ourselves.

So which kind of exercise is the best for weight loss and a fit body? Is it running? Lifting weights? Yoga? The answer is, they are all great. They all move the body. And we encourage you to incorporate a variety of them into your life. Strengthening your arms, conditioning your heart or stretching your hamstrings are all key building blocks of a lean, strong and healthy body.

Stay Motivated and Don't Give Up

Throughout the course of this plan, we have put a lot of emphasis on staying consistent with your daily exercise. The more consistent an action is, the more likely it is to become a habit. Whenever we meet with new clients, we ask questions that give us the ability to help them the best way we can. Often the main struggle when it comes to exercise is, "I just don't have the willpower."

Willpower isn't the answer. It might get you through the first few weeks when it is really necessary. But in order for exercise to become a part of your regular life, you have to make this behavior autopilot. No questioning, no bargaining, no postponing, no constant struggle. It has to be as natural as brushing your teeth every morning.

Let us explain. Let's say that Nikki and I are both on a mission to get healthy.

I am super eager and set out a plan to exercise Mondays, Wednesdays and Fridays. My plan is to get up early and go for a longer walk, lasting about an hour. On Monday, I wake up to

the sound of my alarm clock, put my exercise clothes on and head outside. Without realizing it, I am creating a pattern in my head that associates waking up with exercising.

But on Tuesday, I wake up and don't exercise at all. The pattern linking my daily routine to exercise isn't as strong now. This continues for several weeks and I still need to remind myself to wake up early three times a week and go for my walk. And some days it's a real struggle.

Nikki, on the other hand, plans to exercise every day. She only goes for a half hour fast-paced walk, but she does it every single day. When Nikki's alarm clock sounds, she automatically reaches for her exercise clothes and heads out the door. Her pattern is conditioned repeatedly until it is completely automatic.

The honest truth is that if exercising is a chore, it doesn't matter what you do—you probably won't stick to it long term. During this eight-week plan, you have been introduced to various ways to be active. Our hope is that you continue with the exercise schedule we have put together for you and continue to build a solid habit for life.

Here are some practical suggestions that helped us as well as many of our clients to make exercise a daily habit. We hope you will find them helpful too:

Make It Enjoyable

It doesn't matter what you do if you associate the habit of exercise with pain and struggle—you will try to convince yourself to avoid it. On the other hand, if it's fun, you'll look forward to it. That's why in the first few weeks of this plan we focused on pleasure. We asked you to go outside, at your own pace and enjoy the scenery, the fresh morning air, peace and silence, you and your thoughts— time to just feel. What's not to enjoy about this, right? On days when you need an extra push, some great music, a podcast or an audiobook can be super helpful.

Don't Miss Two Straight Days

If you miss a day, don't give up! Try not to miss a day, but if it happens, make a promise and hold yourself accountable, so you don't miss a second day. Sit down with your calendar and physically schedule a regular appointment with yourself. It helps to have regular times, like first thing in the morning or in the evening after the kids go to bed.

Make It Social

Maybe you have been exercising on your own and didn't consider the option of making it a group thing. Many people ignore the social aspect of exercise, maybe because they think it's not necessary. And it's not, except if you're having a hard time forming the habit. In that case, making it social can work wonders. A few options to consider are to sign up for a fitness class or join a volleyball team, running club or yoga studio. Surround yourself with other people who share and support your goals. Being part of a group offers a couple of benefits: it makes it more fun and it gives you a sense of accountability.

WHAT IF I STILL FIND IT DIFFICULT TO STAY MOTIVATED AND CONSISTENT WITH MY EXERCISE AND EATING?

Allow us to help you. In fact, that's what Nikki and I do best. www.activevegetarian.com is here so you don't have to do it alone. From workouts and healthy eating to motivation and encouragement, we are here to serve you.

YOUR WEEK 8 FITNESS ASSIGNMENT

FIT FOR LIFE

Following is your suggested weekly fitness schedule. Make an effort to follow it closely and commit to moving your body every single day.

LIFESTYLE

"To enjoy good health, to bring true happiness to one's family, to bring peace to all, one must first discipline and control one's own mind."

—*Buddha*

Have you noticed how all the habits, tasks and assignments you've been working on flow together?

Each one plays a significant role on your way to success. Did you notice how well they complement one another, and that without one, the rest won't function as well?

Embracing your new eating habits, morning walks in nature and practicing mindfulness are all responsible for your success today. When put into practice together, they will form a solid foundation for a healthy and happy life. It's not a magical diet, endless amounts of exercise or a new self-help book. It comes down to overall nourishment of the body and mind. To us, successful weight loss means that you are now equipped with all the necessary tools to stay on track. You have established a positive relationship with food, a strong daily exercise routine and you've gained the self-control and confidence to handle any possible challenges along the way.

YOUR WEEK #8 fitness schedule*

*arrange walks, workouts and mobility & yoga sessions as needed to fit appropriately into your schedule.

MONDAY	TUESDAY	WEDNESDAY	THURSDAY	FRIDAY	SATURDAY	SUNDAY
WALK 30 minutes + **MOBILITY SESSION** 15 minutes	**INTERVAL WORKOUT** 20 minutes	**WALK** 30 minutes + **MOBILITY SESSION** 15 minutes	**STRENGTH WORKOUT** 20 minutes	**WALK** 30 minutes + **MOBILITY SESSION** 15 minutes	**YOGA SESSION**	**WALK** 30 minutes

YOUR WEEK 8 LIFESTYLE ASSIGNMENT

NUTRITION, FITNESS AND LIFESTYLE—IT'S ALL ONE!

Let's just recap some of the key factors that will keep you on the right track:

Read Your Mission Statement Daily

This is a subtle yet powerful way to overcome tough times. A personal mission statement brings focus and purpose to your life.

Follow a Bedtime Ritual

This ritual positively affects how you sleep, how fresh you wake up and how much energy you will have the next day. Your productivity and motivation is directly linked to this simple habit.

Practice the One-Minute Meditation

This short "time out" is crazy powerful. Regular practice develops a kinder mind and helps you deal with stress, sadness, fear, frustration or any other negative thoughts.

Enjoy Frequent Visits with Nature

Nature is the truest form of medicine. It can heal anxiety and depression. It's a great way to reduce stress, disconnect from everyday worries and soak up some positive energy. Time in nature is time invested in your happiness.

Do Things that Bring You Joy, Every Single Day

Commit to doing at least one thing every day that makes you happy. Schedule it into your calendar if you have to. Don't skip this. Happiness is your responsibility, so create it!

Have an Effective Way to Manage Stress

Stress is a natural part of life. But beyond a certain point, stress can build up and become damaging to your health, your mood, your productivity, your relationships and your quality of life. To stay healthy, lean and fit, you must manage this load and find ways to de-stress.

Be Active and Nourish Your Body

The benefits of balanced plant-based nutrition and regular physical activity go way beyond physical appearance. Weight loss isn't just about going down a dress size or two. It's about improving your life in many significant ways.

Be an Inspiring Example for Those Around You

The best way to influence your loved ones—your partner, parents or coworkers—is to lead by example. By walking your talk, you become a person others want to follow.

WEEK 8 RESOURCES AVAILABLE FOR YOU ON WWW.ACTIVEVEGETARIAN.COM:

- Week #8 Meal Plan and Shopping List
- Mobility Session #6 (video)
- Bodyweight Strength Workout #4 (video)
- My Yoga #3 (video)
- Interval Training Time #2 (video)
- Personal Message from Nikki and Zuzana (video)

SO WHERE DO I GO FROM HERE?

"Now this is not the end. It is not even the beginning of the end. But it is, perhaps, the end of the beginning."

—*Winston Churchill*

We are coming to the end of our eight weeks and you might be wondering what will happen next. Will you be able to follow through with your new lifestyle choices? Will you have the motivation to keep going strong even when life gets in the way? Will you continue your journey of clean, plant-based eating and daily exercise? Those all are valid questions and concerns.

Let's face it—no one feels motivated to exercise or eat healthy all the time. Everyone has experienced days when their motivation is low and they lack the necessary energy to push through. So how do you prevent falling back into old unhealthy habits? How do you make sure that you don't end up gaining back the weight and starting the search for the "next big thing" or "perfect diet" once again?

Over the course of the past seven weeks, Nikki and I have coached you on implementing the basic habits necessary for you to succeed. You have gained the understanding of what it takes to eat a plant-based diet, lose weight, deal with stress and be physically fit. The truth is, once you reach a certain level of knowledge and experience, the missing link is no longer a new exercise program, the perfect nutrition plan or a new supplement to try.

What you might need, instead, is guidance. Someone who can help you determine what to do next, especially when you're stuck. Someone who's there to support you when challenges and difficulties come up. And let's face it, they always do.

So our question for you is this . . . do you have someone in your life who actually knows how to be healthy and enjoy life? Someone who you respect and look up to? An individual who is vibrant enough and fit enough and willing to share his or her "secret"? Do you have someone who can help you work through challenges and overcome road blocks, rather than just telling you to eat less and exercise more?

If you have a good role model in your life right now, someone who you look up to, someone who is already living the life you desire and someone who can mentor you to success, consider yourself very fortunate and make the absolute most of it! If, however, you don't already have a mentor like that, FIND ONE IMMEDIATELY.

You can always count on us!

Nikki and I are here for you and committed to help you live the life you dream of. Our website, www.activevegetarian.com, was created out of a pure love and passion for healthy plant-based living. We have been blessed with the opportunity to share our experience with clients and readers all over the world. It's our offering to help you take back control of your own life, health and happiness. This is what we do best and seeing you succeed is what fulfills us and inspires us to keep evolving.

In fact, we've never been more devoted than we are now to doing our part in sharing the power of a healthy diet, an active lifestyle and inner peace with as many people as we possibly can.

That is the honest truth. Nikki and I have been quietly working on creating our most comprehensive plan yet. If you choose to continue on this journey with us, together we will build on the foundation you have already established. You will have access to regular exercise videos with Nikki and myself as your trainers, new meal plans weekly, step-by-step recipes and inspiration for living an epic, fun life that's good for you and our planet. If you are up for it, we are ready to offer you all the tools necessary to get closer to your dream life.

Come join us at www.activevegetarian.com, where you will find all the material and support you need to stay on track. Over the years, we've helped many clients build healthy lifestyles that make sense for them. Now it's your turn to receive the guidance and care you need to make this real!

Nikki and I want to thank you! Thanks to you, we get to do what we deeply love. We do not take your support lightly. Please know that. We want to keep earning it by delivering even greater value to you and by being even more of an instrument to help you enjoy the life you deserve. You're simply amazing!

Dedicated to your health and well-being,

—Zuzana and Nikki

PART 3

LET'S GET COOKING

MORNINGS

A healthy vegan breakfast can be as simple or as elaborate as you like, from a quick fuel-up to an all-out brunch extravaganza. These are some of our favorite nutritious ways to start the day.

RISE & SHINE

ANTI-INFLAMMATORY - ANTIDEPRESSANT - LIVER SUPPORT

Turmeric and ginger roots are both excellent for fighting inflammation and enhancing your immune system. Together with oranges and lemon, this juice is the best elixir we know for fighting and/or preventing illnesses.

1 SERVING

2 oranges, peeled

2 apples

4 ribs celery

1 lemon, peeled

2-inch (5-cm) piece of ginger

Small piece of fresh turmeric root

Wash all of the produce well. Put all of the ingredients through a juicer and enjoy!

BODYBUILDER

RESTORATIVE - BLOOD BUILDER - STRESS RELIEVING

This juice combination is designed to beautify the skin, hair, nails and eyes, while also working internally to increase organ function by breaking down processed foods and removing heavy metals from the blood.

1 SERVING

6 kale leaves

1 large cucumber

2 apples

¼ pineapple, peeled

1 lemon, peeled

Wash all of the produce well. Put all of the ingredients through a juicer and enjoy!

EVERYONE'S FAVORITE

DECONGESTANT - BONE STRENGTHENING - SKIN BRIGHTENING

Everyone's Favorite juice is packed with beta-carotene and vitamins A, K and C. Beta-carotene is a major antioxidant and helps maintain the tissues surrounding our internal organs. Vitamin K can improve bone health, while vitamins A and C have proven to be essential for keeping our immune systems healthy and strong.

1 SERVING

3 large carrots, peeled and chopped

2 oranges, peeled and separated

2-inch (5-cm) piece of ginger

1 lime, peeled

Wash all of the produce well. Put all of the ingredients through a juicer and enjoy!

PURITY

ATHLETE'S FUEL - CELLULAR RESTORATION - LOWERS CHOLESTEROL

This is a great one if you're new to juicing because of the sweet factor! Beet juice is a blood purifier and an effective anti-inflammatory, and it's also high in vitamins A, B_1, B_2, B_6 and C. Apples contain tons of phytochemicals (plant compounds that prevent disease) and vitamin C.

1 SERVING

1 beetroot, peeled

2 apples

4 ribs celery

2 limes, peeled

Wash all of the produce well. Juice all of the ingredients and enjoy!

GLOWING GREEN

HEAVY METAL DETOX - ALKALIZING - CLEANSING - ANTIAGING

Get your daily dose of dark leafy greens any time of day with this delicious green smoothie. It's low in calories but very filling. Because it contains high amounts of water and fiber, this smoothie will make you feel as if you just ate a full meal. If you're trying to lose weight, green smoothies will help fight hunger and cravings.

1 SERVING

4 cups (1.4 kg) organic greens of your choice (feel free to mix kale, spinach, romaine lettuce)

½ cup (20 g) fresh cilantro

½ cup (20 g) fresh parsley

2 cups (480 ml) filtered water

1 apple, cored and chopped

1 pear, cored and chopped

1 banana, frozen or fresh

1 lemon, juiced

Ice, if desired

Fill your high-speed blender with all of the greens and herbs. Add the water and blend until liquefied. Add the apple, pear and lemon juice and ice if desired. Blend again until smooth and enjoy!

NOTE: This is a huge smoothie that can be divided into 2 servings if desired.

BLUEBERRY PIE

SKIN BEAUTIFIER - CURBS CRAVINGS - DIGESTIVE SUPPORT

Get a jump-start on your daily dose of veggies with this delicious smoothie. Don't be scared by the spinach—the flavor is so mild you won't even notice it's there. The oats add healthy fiber and help to bulk up the smoothie to make it more satisfying.

1 SERVING

1 cup (150 g) blueberries, frozen or fresh

1 handful fresh spinach, washed

1 cup (240 ml) coconut milk

2 tbsp (20 g) oats

2 dates, pitted

½ lemon, juice and zest

Blend all of the ingredients in a high-speed blender until smooth and enjoy!

ACTIVE RECOVERY

ANTIOXIDANT - PROTEIN PACKED - CANCER FIGHTING

This is a healthy breakfast smoothie with the most insane, creamy, sweet and rich banana bread flavor. It's high in protein as well as potassium, magnesium, vitamin C and other nourishing vitamins, minerals and enzymes we need to maintain optimal health.

1 SERVING

1 cup (240 ml) coconut water

1 handful bok choy, washed

1 banana, frozen or fresh

2 dates, pitted

1 tbsp (10 g) hemp seeds

2 tbsp (23 g) plant-based protein powder

Pinch of cinnamon

Blend all of the ingredients in a high-speed blender until smooth and enjoy!

IMMUNE BOOSTER

ANTI-INFLAMMATORY - DIGESTIVE AID - HORMONAL SUPPORT

This vitamin C-rich Immune Booster smoothie is chock-full of the good stuff to keep you healthy as the seasons change. It's packed with vitamins and antioxidants to help keep colds away. Ground flaxseed adds omega-3s, a wonderful way to prevent many serious chronic diseases.

SERVING

1 large carrot, peeled and chopped

1 orange, peeled and separated

1 cup (240 ml) filtered water

6 leaves romaine lettuce, washed and cut

2 tbsp (20 g) ground flaxseed

2 dates, pitted

Tiny piece of ginger, peeled

Blend all of the ingredients in a high-speed blender until smooth and enjoy!

BASIC ALMOND MILK

ALKALIZING - PROTEIN PACKED - ZERO PRESERVATIVES OR ADDITIVES

To make the perfect almond milk at home, all you need is nuts, water, a blender and cheesecloth. Here's how it's done . . .

2 ½ SERVINGS

1 cup (170 g) raw almonds, preferably organic

2 cups (480 ml) filtered water, plus more for soaking

Pinch of sea salt, optional

Soak the almonds for 24 hours in a bowl filled with filtered water. They will plump as they absorb water. Drain the almonds from their soaking water and rinse them thoroughly under cool running water.

Place the almonds in a high-speed blender and cover with the filtered water. Add the salt, if using. Pulse the blender a few times to break up the almonds, then blend continuously for about 2 minutes. The almonds should be broken down and the mixture should have a smooth and creamy texture.

Strain the mixture into a large bowl through a sprout bag, cheesecloth or kitchen towel.

Store the almond milk in clean sealed jars in the refrigerator for up to 2 days.

MOLASSES TURMERIC MILK

STOMACH SOOTHING - FIGHTS INFECTION - ANTI-INFLAMMATORY

Molasses Turmeric Milk is a delicious and inexpensive way to incorporate some healthful nutrients into your day beverage instead of reaching for a supplement. Molasses is high in calcium, iron and potassium, all while having the lowest sugar content of any product made from sugar cane. Turmeric contains loads of nutrients, especially antioxidants and anti-inflammatory compounds, which make this a potent healing drink.

1 SERVING

1 cup (240 ml) Basic Almond Milk (page 71)

1 tbsp (15 ml) blackstrap molasses

½ tsp ground turmeric

¼ tsp ground cinnamon

¼ tsp ground cardamom

Place all of the ingredients in a high-speed blender. Blend on high for 2 minutes and enjoy.

DEEP CHOCOLATE MILK

ENERGIZING - STRENGTHENS ENDURANCE - ANTIOXIDANT

If you loved drinking a cold glass of chocolate milk as a kid, this new and improved superfood chocolate milk recipe might be just for you!

1 SERVING

1 cup (240 ml) Basic Almond Milk (page 71)

1 tbsp (7 g) raw cacao powder

1 tbsp (12 g) cacao nibs

3 dates, pitted

Place all of the ingredients in a high-speed blender. Blend on high for 2 minutes and enjoy.

MATCHA LATTE

METABOLISM BOOSTER · ANTIOXIDANT · DETOXIFYING

This almond milk matcha latte is a powerhouse drink—it fills you with energy and keeps you satisfied for hours. Matcha is also great for supporting a healthy immune system, enhancing metabolism and concentration, calming the mind and assisting the body in its daily detoxification.

1 SERVING

1 cup (240 ml) Basic Almond Milk (page 71)

1 tsp matcha tea powder

1 tbsp (15 ml) maple syrup or stevia, to taste

1 tsp vanilla

Place all of the ingredients in a high-speed blender. Blend on high for 2 minutes and enjoy.

SPICY CINNAMON TONIC

ENERGIZING · ANTIAGING · SUPPORTS KIDNEY AND LIVER

Drinking cinnamon milk helps to warm our bodies and increase circulation throughout. This tonic also helps ease digestive issues like indigestion and cramping. Drink it cold or warm.

1 SERVING

1 cup (240 ml) Basic Almond Milk (page 71)

2 dates, pitted

1 tsp ground cinnamon

Pinch of cayenne pepper

Place all of the ingredients in a high-speed blender. Blend on high for 2 minutes and enjoy.

COCONUT ALMOND YOGURT

RAW - PACKED WITH PROTEIN - HEALTHY PROBIOTICS

A dairy-free, powerful living cultured yogurt and a real treat! It requires some arm work, but trust me—it's all worth it. This Coconut Almond Yogurt is delicious as is or when added to smoothies, sauces or salad dressings!

2 SERVINGS

1 cup (170 g) raw almonds or other nuts, soaked

Water from 1 young Thai coconut

Meat from 2 young Thai coconuts

6 probiotic capsules

Soak the raw almonds in filtered water for 24 hours. Soaking the nuts is crucial as this will activate the dormant enzymes and release the nutrients.

Drain the almonds from their soaking water and rinse them thoroughly under cool running water.

Place the clean almonds, coconut water, young coconut meat and the powder from the priobiotic capsules into a high-speed blender.

Blend until the ingredients form a smooth yogurt-like consistency.

Pour the mixture into two sealable glass jars, filling only ⅔ of the way full. Cover and let sit at least 3 to 4 hours on a warm day and 4 to 6 hours on a cool day. This will allow the probiotics to start to proliferate and break down the yogurt.

The longer you let it sit, the tangier it will be. Store in the refrigerator and enjoy with granola, in smoothies, in salad dressings or eat it plain.

EASY GRANOLA

NUTRITIONALLY RICH - SATISFYING - MAKES A HEALTHY SNACK

Making your own granola at home is super easy and quick and allows you to control the amount of sugar and quality of ingredients while also changing things up and adding in the flavors that you love. Be creative and experiment with different dried fruits, nuts and seeds. Just remember to use raw, organic ingredients whenever possible.

6 SERVINGS

2 cups (161 g) old-fashioned rolled oats

½ cup (58 g) raw nuts and/or seeds, soaked and rinsed (walnuts, pumpkin seeds, sunflower seeds)

½ cup (75 g) dried fruit, chopped if large (dates, raisins, apricots)

½ tsp Himalayan sea salt

½ tsp ground cinnamon

½ tsp ground ginger

¼ cup (60 ml) melted coconut oil

¼ cup (60 ml) maple syrup

1 tsp vanilla extract

1 organic lemon, juice and zest

Optional additional mix-ins: 2 tbsp (23 g) cacao nibs or ¼ cup (19 g) coconut flakes

Preheat the oven to 350°F (177°C) and line a large baking tray with parchment paper.

In a large mixing bowl, combine the oats, nuts and/or seeds, dried fruit, salt, cinnamon and ginger. Stir to mix all ingredients.

In a separate bowl, mix the melted coconut oil, maple syrup, vanilla, lemon juice and zest. Pour over the dry ingredients and mix well. Spread the granola on your prepared pan and use a large spoon to form an even layer. Bake until golden, about 20 to 24 minutes, stirring once or twice to make sure that the edges don't burn.

Allow the granola to cool completely; it will further crisp up as it cools down. Mix in any additional goodies, such as cacao nibs or coconut.

Store the granola in an airtight container at room temperature for 1 to 2 weeks

You can also store granola sealed in a freezer bag in the freezer for up to 2 months.

CHIA PUDDING BASE

ANTIAGING · PROTEIN RICH · CURBS HUNGER

Chia seeds are a powerhouse of nutrients, containing omega-3 fatty acids, protein, fiber and minerals, including calcium—up to three times more than a serving of milk. The seeds also expand in liquid, which helps provide a pudding-like consistency and gives you a satisfied, full feeling—and a shot of energy!

2 SERVINGS

⅓ cup (53 g) chia seeds

2 cups (480 ml) nondairy milk, such as almond or coconut

Mix the two ingredients until well combined. Cover with a plate and allow the mixture to sit for at least 20 minutes or preferably overnight. During this time, the seeds with excrete a gel and the liquid will thicken.

In the morning, stir the chia pudding carefully. If it's too thin, add in more chia seeds, 1 tablespoon (10 g) at a time, to thicken. If it's too thick, add in more milk, 1 tablespoon (15 ml) at a time, to thin.

To make this ahead of time, cover and refrigerate for up to 2 days.

BANANA CHOCOLATE PIE

ENERGY BOOSTER · DIGESTIVE SUPPORT · LOWERS CHOLESTEROL

Chocolate and banana is such an amazingly delicious combination and perfect for a luxurious chia breakfast like this!

2 SERVINGS

¼ cup (28 g) unsweetened cacao powder

2 tbsp (30 ml) maple syrup

Chia Pudding Base (page 78)

1 large banana, thinly sliced

1 tbsp (12 g) cacao nibs, for garnish

Add the cacao powder and some maple syrup to your chia pudding base and mix it all together. If the pudding is too dry, add a few tablespoons of almond or coconut milk.

Divide the chocolate pudding evenly between 2 jars and arrange the sliced bananas over the top of each serving. Garnish with the cacao nibs and enjoy.

PUMPKIN SPICE CHIA PUDDING

HIGH IN CALCIUM - MUSCLE REPAIR - HEART AND LIVER HEALTH

This pudding is velvety smooth and tastes like pumpkin pie! It's protein-rich and makes a great light snack, dessert or breakfast. Yes, this means you can eat pie for breakfast.

2 SERVINGS

1 cup (180 g) pumpkin puree

1 tsp pumpkin pie spice

3 tbsp (45 ml) maple syrup

Chia Pudding Base (page 78)

1 tbsp (10 g) hemp seeds, for garnish

1 tbsp (10 g) organic lemon zest, for garnish

Add the pumpkin puree, pumpkin pie spice and maple syrup to the chia pudding base. Mix well, garnishing with the hemp seeds and organic lemon zest.

BERRY LIME PUDDING

STRENGTHENS IMMUNE SYSTEM - HEALTHY SKIN, NAILS AND HAIR

The brain-boosting omega-3s in the berries combined with fiber and protein from the chia seeds make this pudding a great breakfast option or naturally sweet treat. Packed with nutrients and protein, it delivers long-lasting energy with every spoonful.

2 SERVINGS

Chia Pudding Base (page 78)

2 tbsp (30 ml) maple syrup

½ lime, juice and zest

½ tsp ground vanilla or vanilla extract

2 cups (250 g) fresh ripe raspberries
(or thawed frozen)

Mix the chia pudding base with the maple syrup, lime juice and vanilla.

In two jars or bowls, layer the chia pudding and raspberries. Garnish with the lime zest and enjoy.

COCONUT MANGO PUDDING

HELPS TREAT DIABETES - PROMOTES HEALTHY DIGESTION - PREVENTS ANEMIA

Tropical, refreshing, summery and healthy. What more could you want?

2 SERVINGS

4 tbsp (19 g) shredded coconut

2 tbsp (30 ml) maple syrup

¼ tsp ground cinnamon

¼ tsp ground cardamom

Chia Pudding Base (page 78)

1 fresh mango, diced

Add the coconut, maple syrup and spices into your chia pudding base and mix well.

Divide half of this mixture evenly between 2 jars. Layer some diced fresh mango on top of the pudding layer. Alternate layers of chia pudding and freshly diced mango until the jars are filled to the top, ending with freshly diced mango. Garnish with extra shredded coconut and enjoy.

OVERNIGHT MAPLE WALNUT OATS

SATISFYING - STABILIZES BLOOD SUGAR - GOOD FOR THE BRAIN

Meet the easiest breakfast of all time: overnight oats. It does not get any better than mixing a few ingredients together before bed and grabbing a spoon when you're ready to eat a delicious, healthy breakfast.

1 SERVING

½ cup (40 g) old-fashioned oats, gluten-free

1 tsp chia seeds

2 tbsp (15 g) raw walnuts, chopped

½ cup (120 ml) unsweetened almond milk

1 tbsp (15 ml) pure maple syrup, more or less to taste

Small pinch of salt

Toppings, such as hemp seeds, ground flaxseed, sliced banana, cacao nibs, etc.

Place all of the ingredients in a jar, shake, cover and refrigerate overnight. The next morning, add your favorite toppings and enjoy!

ZOATS

Zoats—zucchini mixed with oats—make a healthy start to any day. Leave the zucchini skin on to benefit from the soluble fiber, which slows down digestion, keeping your insulin levels even and you feeling fuller for longer.

2 SERVINGS

½ cup (40 g) old-fashioned oats, gluten-free

1 small organic zucchini, grated

1 cup (240 ml) almond milk, homemade or unsweetened

½ cup (120 ml) water

½ tsp vanilla extract

2 tsp (5 g) raw cacao powder

½ tbsp (7.5 ml) maple syrup or stevia, to taste

1 scoop raw plant-based protein powder (We prefer RAW Organic Protein, Chocolate Cacao by Garden of Life)

Sliced bananas and cacao nibs, for garnish

Mix the oats, zucchini, almond milk, water, vanilla, cacao powder and maple syrup in a small saucepan and cook for about 8 to 10 minutes on medium heat.

Remove from the heat and slowly mix in the protein powder, stirring to prevent clumping.

Serve with the sliced bananas and cacao nibs, if desired.

THE ULTIMATE VEGAN BREAKFAST SANDWICH

VERY NUTRITIOUS - GOOD FOR THE BONES - GREAT SOURCE OF IRON

If you prefer savory breakfasts, this is the sandwich for you. You can use any kind of mushrooms and herbs for this recipe, and it'll taste absolutely delicious.

2 SERVINGS

2 tbsp (30 ml) coconut oil

½ large onion, chopped

2 cloves garlic, chopped

1 large tomato, chopped

8 organic button mushrooms, sliced

1 tsp oregano

Salt and black pepper to taste

Small bunch of cilantro leaves, finely chopped

½ avocado, mashed

2 sprouted-grain English muffins, toasted (can substitute with 4 sprouted-grain bread slices)

Homemade Ketchup (page 171)

Heat a skillet to medium heat and add the oil. Add the onion and sauté until tender, about 5 to 7 minutes. Add the chopped garlic and sauté until fragrant, about a minute.

Add the chopped tomato, sliced mushrooms, oregano and salt and pepper and sauté until they start to caramelize and turn golden brown, about 10 to 15 minutes.

Add in the chopped cilantro, give it one more stir, turn the heat off and set the skillet aside. Spread the mashed avocado evenly on the toasted English muffin, covering only the bottom side. Top the avocado with half of the mushroom mixture and any additional veggies of your choice.

Finish it with the remaining half of the muffin. Serve with Homemade Ketchup (page 171).

CHEESY SCRAMBLED TEMPEH AND GREENS

MUSCLE-BUILDING - SUPPORTS DIGESTIVE HEALTH - RICH IN B VITAMINS

This scramble can be enjoyed as a quick meal or served on a sprouted-grain tortilla as a burrito. You could also add black beans, guacamole and more veggies for a perfect go-to dinner for busy weeknights.

2 SERVINGS

1 tbsp (15 ml) coconut oil

½ onion, chopped

¼ tsp cumin seeds

1 tsp ground turmeric

6 oz (170 g) plain tempeh, crumbled

4 collard greens, stemmed
and chopped

4–6 cherry tomatoes, cut in half

4 tbsp (60 ml) almond milk

1 tbsp (10 g) nutritional yeast

Heat the coconut oil in a skillet and sauté the onion together with the cumin seeds and turmeric for about 5 minutes. Add a bit of water if needed.

Mix in the crumbled tempeh and collard greens and continue to cook for another 8 to 10 minutes. Toss in the cherry tomatoes and cook for another 1 to 2 minutes.

Turn the heat to low and stir in the almond milk and nutritional yeast. Mix well and cook for 1 to 2 minutes.

Serve with Basic Green Salad (page 91), tomatoes and a sprouted-grain tortilla.

LUNCHTIME

These healthy lunch recipes include make-ahead salads, healthy sandwiches and low-carb veggie noodles. We chose quick and tasty meals to help you make the most of your lunch break (and stay away from fast food).

NUTTY LIME CARROT SALAD

IMMUNE BOOSTER - DIGESTION AID - HEART HEALTHY

One of our simplest and yummiest salads to make! Eat it on its own, as a side dish or stuffed inside collard wraps.

2-3 SERVINGS

5 medium organic carrots

¼ cup (38 g) soaked organic raisins

2 tbsp (20 g) pumpkin seeds

2 tbsp (20 g) sunflower seeds

1 tbsp (10 g) hemp seeds

¼ cup (10 g) chopped fresh cilantro

DRESSING

¼ cup (45 g) raw almond butter

1 tbsp (15 ml) coconut aminos

1 lime, juiced

¼-inch (6-mm) piece of ginger, optional

If your food processor has a grating blade, this is the quickest method. Simply wash and cut the ends off of the carrots and shred them in a food processor. Otherwise, grate them by hand.

Place the shredded carrots in a large bowl. Add the raisins, pumpkin seeds, sunflower seeds, hemp seeds and fresh cilantro.

In a blender, combine all of the dressing ingredients and blend well. If it is too thick, add some almond milk to thin it out.

Pour the dressing over the salad and stir until well combined.

BASIC GREEN SALAD

NUTRIENT DENSE - LOADED WITH VITAMIN C - ALKALIZING

The Basic Green Salad is a great start to an amazing salad. Mix and match with a variety of seasonal ingredients and top it with any dressings, dips or sauces from this book. Be creative—the possibilities are endless.

2 SERVINGS

1 head organic romaine lettuce, chopped

2 cups (40 g) organic baby arugula

1 cup (16 g) fresh cilantro, chopped

1 cup (60 g) fresh parsley, chopped

Combine all of the greens in a big salad bowl. Eat the salad fresh or store in a closed container in the refrigerator for 1 to 2 days.

SWEET & SAVORY GREEN SALAD

PROMOTES WEIGHT LOSS · REMOVES TOXINS · HIGH IN ANTIOXIDANTS

A light, healthy and easy-to-assemble salad for all occasions!

1 SERVING

2–3 cups (80–120 g) Basic Green Salad (page 91) or any leafy greens of your choice

½ ripe avocado, diced

¼ cup (40 g) blueberries, rinsed and dried

¼ cucumber, peeled and diced

2 tbsp (13 g) dried cranberries (preferably unsweetened)

⅓ cup (80 ml) Easy Vinaigrette Dressing (page 169)

½ cup (20 g) mixed sprouts (alfalfa, lentil, clover, etc.)

Add the Basic Green Salad, avocado, blueberries, cucumber and cranberries together in a large bowl.

Drizzle evenly with the Easy Vinaigrette Dressing. Gently toss until the salad is combined and evenly coated. Top with sprouts and enjoy.

BEET, ORANGE & APPLE SALAD

NUTRIENT DENSE · LOADED WITH VITAMIN C · ALKALIZING

Sweet, tart, salty goodness in every single bite. The added pumpkin seeds makes for a delicious and nutritious combination.

2 SERVINGS

2–3 cups (80–120 g) Basic Green Salad (page 91) or any leafy greens of your choice

1 small orange, peeled and sliced into rounds

½ apple, cored and diced

½ small beet, peeled and shredded

¼ cup (40 g) raw pumpkin seeds

⅓ cup (80 ml) Miso Ginger Dressing (page 170)

Fresh black pepper, if desired

Add the Basic Green Salad, orange, apple, beet and pumpkin seeds together in a large bowl. Drizzle evenly with the Miso Ginger Dressing, and gently toss until the salad is combined and evenly coated.

Serve immediately, topped with some freshly cracked black pepper if desired.

ROASTED GARLIC AND RED PEPPER SANDWICH

BOOSTS IMMUNE SYSTEM - SUPPORTS WEIGHT LOSS - EASILY DIGESTIBLE

Combining garlic and roasted red peppers gives this sandwich an amazing flavor. It makes a delicious and nutritious lunch.

2 SERVINGS

2 red bell peppers

4 cloves garlic, peeled

1 tsp extra virgin olive oil

4 slices sprouted-grain sandwich bread

4 tbsp (30 g) Honest Sour Cream (page 175)

6 fresh basil leaves

Sea salt and freshly ground pepper, to taste

Optional toppings: red onion, sprouts, avocado and spinach

Preheat the oven to 450°F (233°C). Line a small baking sheet with aluminum foil.

Wash the bell peppers, leaving their stems intact. Place the garlic cloves in a small piece of aluminum foil, drizzle with olive oil and wrap into a small ball. Place the wrapped garlic and peppers on the prepared baking sheet, leaving a bit of space between them.

Roast in the oven, checking every 5 minutes or so. Turn peppers as they begin to brown. Keep turning until the skin is blistered and black and the peppers are soft but not completely falling apart, about 30 to 35 minutes. Allow to cool.

Cut the peppers in half, scrape out the ribs and seeds and peel off the skin. Carefully unwrap the garlic and mash it into a paste.

Toast the bread. Spread each piece with 1 tablespoon (7.5 g) of sour cream. On top of the sour cream on one half of the bread, add 3 basil leaves, garlic paste and red pepper. Sprinkle with salt and pepper.

Add any additional toppings of choice, cover with the other slice of bread and enjoy!

MEDITERRANEAN QUINOA GREEN SALAD

SATISFYING - PROTEIN RICH - GOOD SOURCE OF IRON

This is a big, colorful bowl of healthy, crunchy goodness. It's light but filling, healthy and bursting with fresh flavors. This salad packs great for later; just store the dressing separately and toss just before serving.

1 SERVING

2–3 cups (80–120 g) Basic Green Salad (page 91) or any leafy greens of your choice

¼ cup (40 g) quinoa, cooked

¼ cup (50 g) chickpeas, rinsed

6 sun-dried olives, pitted and chopped

10 cherry tomatoes, diced

⅓ cup (80 ml) Creamy Red Pepper Sauce (page 169)

Add the Basic Green Salad, quinoa, chickpeas, olives and cherry tomatoes together in a large bowl. Pour the Creamy Red Pepper Sauce over the salad, gently toss until combined and evenly coated and enjoy.

NOTE: **There is a difference between a green olive and a black sun-ripened one. Ripened black olives contain more nutrients, more olive oil and are far healthier to eat.**

CURRY QUINOA SALAD

EASY TO DIGEST - PROTEIN PACKED - HIGH IN IRON AND MAGNESIUM

This is a satisfying salad to make ahead for a busy week and also a great choice to bring to a potluck with friends or family.

4 SERVINGS

¼ cup (43 g) raw organic whole almonds

¼ cup (40 g) raw pumpkin seeds

1 cup (170 g) organic white quinoa

1 tbsp (15 ml) maple syrup

1 tbsp (10 g) finely chopped shallot

1 tsp curry powder

¼ tsp coarse salt

2 tbsp (30 ml) fresh lemon juice

Freshly ground pepper

2 tbsp (30 ml) extra virgin olive oil

2 tbsp (13 g) unsweetened dried cranberries

1 small organic apple, cut into small chunks

Preheat the oven to 375°F (191°C). Spread the almonds and pumpkin seeds on a baking sheet and bake until lightly toasted and fragrant, about 7 minutes. Let cool before coarsely chopping the nuts.

Rinse the quinoa thoroughly and drain. Bring 2 cups (480 ml) of water to a boil in a medium saucepan. Add the quinoa and return to a boil. Stir the quinoa, cover and reduce heat. Simmer until the quinoa is tender but still chewy, about 15 minutes. Fluff the quinoa with a fork; let cool.

Whisk together the maple syrup, shallot, curry powder, salt and lemon juice in a large bowl. Season with pepper. Whisking constantly, slowly add the oil and whisk until the dressing is well combined. Add the quinoa, cranberries, apple, seeds and nuts; toss well. Serve as is or use as a stuffing for collard wraps.

KALE CAESAR SALAD

DETOXIFYING - ANTI-INFLAMMATORY - EXCELLENT SOURCE OF VITAMIN C

Kale is the king of leafy greens and one of the most nutrient-dense foods you can eat. It's rich in vitamins and minerals and is packed with powerful antioxidants that can help lower cholesterol. This salad is tossed with vegan Caesar dressing and topped with roasted chickpeas.

1 SERVING AS MAIN MEAL OR 2 SIDE SALADS

1 large bunch organic kale

1 tsp flax oil

½ lemon, juiced

½ cup (50 g) Lemon Pepper Roasted Chickpeas (page 141)

2 tbsp (23 g) Vegan Parmesan (page 177)

DRESSING

2 tbsp (23 g) tahini

2 tbsp (20 g) hemp seeds

1 tbsp (10 g) nutritional yeast

1 date, pitted

½ lemon, juiced

1 tsp organic lemon zest

½ tsp Dijon mustard

1 garlic clove

¼ cup (60 ml) water

1 tsp kelp granules, optional

Salt and pepper, to taste

Wash the kale leaves thoroughly, then remove the stems. Tear the leaves into small pieces. In a large bowl, add the kale, flax oil and lemon juice and massage for about 2 minutes. This helps the kale to break down and makes it easier to digest.

Add all of the dressing ingredients to a high-speed blender and blend on high until smooth and creamy. Transfer to a glass jar.

When ready to eat the salad, pour the dressing over the kale, tossing to coat evenly. Portion out the dressed kale to your serving dishes and top each salad with roasted chickpeas and the vegan Parmesan cheese.

Serve with a wedge of lemon.

CHICKPEA SALAD SANDWICH

SATISFYING - AIDS DIGESTION - HEALTHY FATS

Full of texture and flavor, this is a hearty sandwich that will comfort you and leave you feeling completely satisfied.

2 SERVINGS

1 (15-oz [425-g]) can chickpeas, rinsed and drained

1 ripe avocado

2 tbsp (13 g) dried cranberries

1 shallot, peeled and chopped into small pieces

1 rib organic celery, cut into small pieces

½ lemon, juiced

Sea salt, to taste

4 slices sprouted-grain sandwich bread

Optional toppings: sprouts, tomato, pickles and lettuce

In a medium bowl, smash the chickpeas with a fork. Add in the avocado and keep smashing until the avocado is smooth, leaving a few chunky pieces.

Mix in the cranberries, shallot, celery and lemon juice. Season with salt to taste.

Toast the slices of sandwich bread. Add a layer of chickpea salad to 2 of the slices. Top the chickpea salad with the toppings of your choice and the remaining slices of bread.

Chickpea filling can be stored in the refrigerator for up to 3 days. It can also be used to top salads or to stuff collard wraps.

TEMPEH REUBEN SANDWICH

PROTEIN PACKED - HEALTHY PROBIOTICS - SUPPORTS BONE STRENGTH

The hearty flavor of the tempeh combined with the tanginess of the sauerkraut and creaminess of the vegan cheese makes this a delicious sandwich. Tempeh is loaded with fiber, which makes it even better for digestion. It's also a good source of protein, vitamin B$_2$ and magnesium. Plus, the sauerkraut is fermented, so it's a great way to double up on your fermented-food action and line your digestive system with good bacteria.

2 SERVINGS

8 oz (225 g) tempeh, unflavored

2 tsp (10 ml) sesame seed oil

2 tsp (10 ml) coconut aminos

1 cup (225 g) sauerkraut, drained, lightly rinsed and liquid squeezed out

4 slices sprouted-grain sandwich bread, toasted

Optional toppings: sprouts, tomato, pickles and arugula

6 tbsp (92 g) "Thrive" Cheeze Sauce (page 174)

In a small bowl, marinate the tempeh in the sesame seed oil and coconut aminos for at least 20 minutes. Throw it on a grill and cook for 5 minutes or, if using a stovetop, cook over medium heat for 3 minutes on each side.

Distribute the sauerkraut evenly over 2 slices of bread and place the grilled tempeh over sauerkraut.

Add any additional toppings of your choice, and pour 3 tablespoons (46 g) of the cheese sauce over each sandwich. Top with another slice of bread.

Serve alone or with a Basic Green Salad (page 91).

PORTOBELLO VEGGIE SANDWICH

RICH IN B VITAMINS - BOOSTS IMMUNE SYSTEM - GREAT SOURCE OF PROTEIN

Well-seasoned and grilled portobello mushrooms are a perfect plant-based substitute for meat. This sandwich makes a quick, simple, healthy comfort food for lunch or dinner.

2 SERVINGS

2 large portobello mushroom caps

Handful of arugula

4 slices sprouted-grain sandwich bread, toasted

1 large tomato

1 cup (135 g) alfalfa sprouts

MARINADE

1 tbsp (15 ml) extra virgin olive oil

¼ cup (38 g) finely chopped onion

2 cloves garlic, minced

1 medium tomato, cut into quarters

2 tbsp (30 ml) lemon juice

2 tbsp (30 g) fresh peeled ginger, minced

2 tbsp (30 ml) coconut aminos

1 tbsp (15 ml) maple syrup

2 dates, pitted

½ tsp salt, or to taste

Remove and discard the stems from the mushrooms. Using a small spoon, scrape out and discard the gills. Gently wipe the mushroom caps with a damp paper towel and transfer them to a sealable glass container.

In a blender, combine all of the marinade ingredients and blend for 1 to 3 minutes or until smooth. Pour the marinade over the mushroom caps, coating well. Allow the mushrooms to marinate at least 15 minutes, or up to 1 hour.

Preheat your oven to 425°F (218°C).

Place the mushroom caps on a baking sheet. Brush both sides with the remaining marinade and place the mushrooms cap-side up.

Roast the mushrooms for 15 minutes. Using tongs, flip the mushrooms so the gill side is now up and place back in the oven for an additional 5 minutes. Remove the baking sheet from the oven.

Assemble the sandwich by adding some arugula on the bottom slice of lightly toasted sprouted-grain bread, then layer the portobello, tomato and sprouts.

Top up with the other slice of bread and enjoy!

ZOODLES, AKA ZUCCHINI NOODLES

WEIGHT LOSS SUPPORT - HIGH IN VITAMIN C - EYE HEALTH

Zucchini noodles are an awesome alternative to starchy pasta. They are low-carb, low-calorie, vegan and gluten-free. This light dish is quick to prepare, easily digested, satisfying and guilt-free.

Spiralized zucchini can be stored in the refrigerator for up to 3 days, making it easy to prepare ahead. Place the zoodles in a glass container with a paper towel at the bottom to help absorb any excess moisture, cover with a lid and store in the refrigerator until ready to eat.

1 SERVING = 1 LARGE ZUCCHINI

1 large zucchini

1 tbsp (15 ml) extra virgin olive oil (for cooked version)

1 garlic clove, minced (for cooked version)

SAUCES

Sun-Dried Tomato Basil Marinara Sauce (page 171)

Herbalicious Pesto (page 172)

"Thrive" Cheeze Sauce (page 174)

Creamy Red Pepper Sauce (page 169)

Rinse the zucchini well, pat it dry and chop the ends off, so you have a flat end on either side. Using a spiralizer or julienne peeler, slice the zucchini into noodles.

For a raw dish, place the zoodles into a large serving bowl. Pour sauce over the zoodles and enjoy.

To cook the zoodles, heat the olive oil in a large skillet over medium-high heat. Add the garlic and cook until the garlic is fragrant, about 2 to 3 minutes. Add the zoodles and sauté for 2 minutes. Do not overcook, as zoodles will become mushy!

Remove from heat, top with the sauce of your choice and serve.

DINNER

Who knew vegetables could taste so good? Our dinner dishes are bold, innovative, fresh, easy and, above all, delicious.

MISO SOUP

CANCER-FIGHTING PROBIOTICS - IMPROVES DIGESTION - SOURCE OF VITAMIN K

Miso soup is a delicious bowl of health and antiaging power. Miso not only makes you feel good, it's also very good for you—it's a great source of antioxidants, dietary fiber and protein.

4 SERVINGS

1 tsp toasted sesame oil

½ red onion, finely sliced

Thumb-size piece of ginger, minced

2 cloves garlic, minced

5 cups (1 L) filtered water

1 carrot, peeled

1 cup (170 g) broccoli florets

6 mushrooms, quartered

¼ cup (6.5 g) dried seaweed (or 1 sheet nori seaweed, cut into thin strips)

½ cup (75 g) green peas

3 tsp (15 g) miso paste

1 heaping cup (40 g) baby leaf spinach, chopped

Sesame seeds, for garnish, optional

2 spring onions, finely chopped, for garnish, optional

In a large pot, heat the sesame oil over medium heat. Add in the sliced onion and cook for several minutes, stirring often. After a few minutes, add in the minced ginger and garlic and stir on low heat. Add the water, carrot, broccoli and mushrooms and bring to a simmer. Cover and simmer for 15 minutes, or until veggies are tender. Add the seaweed and peas and cook for another 5 minutes.

Place the miso paste in a bowl and add about ½ cup (120 ml) of warm water. Stir or whisk until there are no clumps. Add the miso mixture to the soup and heat through but do not boil. Taste, adding more miso if needed.

Add the fresh spinach and stir. Serve immediately topped with sesame seeds and spring onions.

HUMMUS SOUP

PROTEIN PACKED · HELPS LOWER CHOLESTEROL · GREAT SOURCE OF CALCIUM

That's right—we turned the dip of the decade into a soup that's savory, silky and garlicky good. In this recipe, chickpeas, carrots and seasonings are blended into a creamy puree. Even if you're inexperienced in the kitchen, everyone will be impressed with the results.

MAKES 4 CUP-SIZE SERVINGS OR 2 LARGE BOWL SERVINGS

1 cup (200 g) dried chickpeas or 2 (15-oz [425-g]) cans chickpeas (drained and rinsed)

1 tbsp (14 g) coconut oil

½ onion, chopped

2 cloves garlic, minced

1 tsp smoked paprika

1 tsp ground turmeric

Salt and fresh pepper, to taste

2 carrots, peeled and chopped

2 tbsp (30 ml) coconut aminos

2 cups (480 ml) filtered water

3 tbsp (34 g) tahini

1 organic lemon, juiced and peeled

Optional garnish: chopped cilantro, cooked or roasted chickpeas, lemon juice and paprika

If using dried beans, soak them overnight. Drain and rinse. Cook for about 90 minutes.

In a large pot, melt the coconut oil. Add in the chopped onion and cook over medium heat for 5 minutes, stirring often. Add in the minced garlic and stir on low heat for an additional 3 minutes.

Add in paprika, turmeric, salt and freshly ground pepper. Stir for another minute or two, being careful not to burn, adding a little bit of water if necessary.

Add in the chickpeas, carrots, coconut aminos and water. Stir well and bring to a boil. Reduce heat to simmer for another 15 to 20 minutes or until the carrots are tender.

Turn off the heat, and carefully transfer the soup into a high-speed blender. Add in the tahini, lemon juice and lemon peel.

Blend until smooth. Be very careful opening the blender as it could explode and splash you.

Pour into bowls and serve with garnish.

SLOW COOKER TURNIP & FENNEL SOUP

RELIEVES CONGESTION - ANTI-INFLAMMATORY - PROMOTES WEIGHT LOSS

A perfect soup to come home to on a chilly night. Rutabaga, also known as yellow turnip, has a lovely sweet flavor and is great roasted, sautéed or cooked. If you're a little afraid of fennel, this is a great way to ease into the flavor, since it's very subtle here.

MAKES 4 CUP-SIZE SERVINGS OR 2 LARGE BOWL SERVINGS

1 tbsp (14 g) coconut oil

1 onion, chopped

4 cloves garlic, minced

1 thumb-sized piece of ginger, minced

½ tbsp (5 g) fennel seeds

½ tsp sea salt

½ tsp black pepper

3 cups (720 ml) filtered water

1 large yellow turnip, peeled and cubed

1 bulb fresh fennel, chopped, divided

½ tsp ground cumin

½ tsp ground cinnamon

¼ tsp ground cardamom

1 (15-oz [425-g]) can full-fat coconut milk (about 1½ cups [360 ml])

½ cup (80 g) hemp seeds, for garnish

½ cup (20 g) fresh cilantro, finely chopped, for garnish

In a skillet, melt the oil over medium heat. Add the onion and cook, stirring until softened, about 3 minutes. Add the garlic, ginger, fennel seeds and salt and pepper and stir until the garlic is fragrant, about 2 to 3 minutes.

Transfer to a slow cooker. Stir in the filtered water. Add the turnip, fennel, cumin, cinnamon and cardamom to the slow cooker, stirring so all of the ingredients are well coated with the spices.

Cover and cook on low for 6 hours or on high for 3 hours, until the turnip is tender.

Stir in the coconut milk and puree the soup using an immersion blender in the slow cooker, or transfer the soup to a high-speed blender and blend in batches if necessary. Season to taste with sea salt.

Ladle the soup into bowls and garnish with hemp seeds and chopped cilantro.

CHEEZY BROCCOLI SOUP

GREAT SOURCE OF B$_{12}$ - ANTIOXIDANT - GREAT SOURCE OF VITAMIN K

This thick and creamy broccoli soup is lick-the-bowl good! Pure comfort that is ready in under 30 minutes. You can always make it ahead of time too and store it in the refrigerator for a few days, as the flavor gets even better the next day.

MAKES 4 CUP-SIZE SERVINGS OR 2 LARGE BOWL SERVINGS

2 tbsp (28 g) coconut oil

1 medium red onion, diced

3 cloves garlic, minced

1 tsp sea salt

1 tsp black pepper

1 tsp Dijon mustard

2½ cups (592 ml) Basic Almond Milk (page 71)

2½ cups (600 ml) filtered water

2 tbsp (30 ml) coconut aminos

5 cups (1 kg) broccoli florets

1 cup (151 g) nutritional yeast

1 tbsp (15 ml) lemon juice

In a large pot, melt the coconut oil. Add in the diced onion and heat over medium for 5 minutes, stirring often. Add the garlic, salt and pepper and Dijon mustard and cook for 2 minutes.

Add the milk, water, coconut aminos and broccoli and bring to a simmer. Cover and cook for about 20 minutes or until the broccoli is tender.

Turn off the heat and stir in the nutritional yeast and lemon juice. Remove the soup and puree in a blender.

Pour the soup back into the pot to keep warm until serving.

WHOLESOME PORTOBELLO STEW

CANCER PREVENTION · GREAT PROTEIN SOURCE · BONE BUILDER

The very best in comfort food—portobello stew. Hearty, delicious and simple, just the way it should be. And it comes with many health benefits.

3–4 SERVINGS

2 tbsp (30 ml) coconut oil, divided

1 medium white onion, chopped

1 tsp dried rosemary

1 tsp dried thyme

1 tsp sweet paprika

2–3 cloves garlic

2 organic portobello mushrooms, stemmed and thinly sliced

2 bay leaves

½ cup (120 ml) balsamic vinegar

3 medium carrots, chopped

2 medium sweet potatoes, chopped

2 ribs celery, chopped

1 cup (166 g) tempeh, crumbled

1 tbsp (15 ml) coconut aminos

1 tsp sea salt

Cracked black pepper

3 cups (720 ml) filtered water

2 tbsp (17 g) spelt flour (or any other gluten-free flour)

Fresh parsley for garnish, optional

Heat 1 tablespoon (15 ml) of oil in large skillet over medium heat. Add the onion, rosemary, thyme and sweet paprika, and cook for 6 to 8 minutes. Add the garlic, stirring occasionally, and cook for another 2 minutes or until lightly browned.

Remove from the heat and transfer the mixture to a bowl.

Return the pan to medium heat and add the remaining 1 tablespoon (15 ml) of oil. When the pan is hot, add the portobello mushrooms and bay leaves, cover with a lid and sauté until nicely browned, about 5 minutes, adding a few tablespoons of water if needed.

Pour the balsamic vinegar over the mushrooms and simmer on very low heat for another 3 to 5 minutes. Add the onion mixture, carrots, sweet potatoes, celery, crumbled tempeh, coconut aminos, salt, black pepper and water, and bring to a boil.

Simmer gently 20 to 25 minutes or until vegetables are tender. Turn the heat to low.

In a small bowl, mix the spelt flour with 1 cup (240 ml) of water, whisking together until the flour is integrated and forms a cloudy fluid. Add the flour and water to the stew, stirring to combine well. Cook for another 5 to 10 minutes, until the flour thickens the stew.

Remove from the heat. Serve with fresh chopped parsley as a garnish.

HEARTY LENTIL STEW

WEIGHT MANAGEMENT · RICH IN PROTEIN · SOURCE OF IRON

A thick and hearty lentil stew, this dish is low in fat and high in fiber, protein and iron. Plus, it's made with comforting Indian spices and ready in under 30 minutes.

3–4 SERVINGS

1 tbsp (14 g) coconut oil

1 small onion, diced

1 tsp minced ginger

2 cloves garlic, minced

1 medium carrot, diced

1 cup (200 g) dry red lentils, rinsed and drained

2 medium tomatoes, diced

6 tbsp (100 g) tomato paste

3½ cups (840 ml) filtered water

½ tsp garam masala

1 tsp ground coriander

1 tsp ground turmeric

1 cinnamon stick, optional

Salt and pepper, to taste

¼ cup (60 ml) full-fat coconut milk

Chopped cilantro, for garnish

In a large skillet, melt the coconut oil and sauté the onion and ginger over medium heat for 5 to 6 minutes. Stir frequently and add a tiny amount of water to the pan if necessary.

Add the garlic and carrot, and sauté for another 3 minutes. Add the lentils, tomatoes, tomato paste, water, garam masala, coriander, turmeric, cinnamon stick and salt and pepper.

Bring to a simmer over medium heat. Then reduce the heat to medium-low and let it simmer for 25 minutes or until the lentils are cooked.

Stir in the coconut milk and let it simmer for 2 minutes.

Garnish with cilantro and serve.

AFRICAN STEW WITH LENTILS, KALE AND YAMS

GOOD PROTEIN SOURCE - LOW-GLYCEMIC - GOOD SOURCE OF VITAMIN B COMPLEX

A play on traditional African peanut stew, this soup substitutes almond butter for a healthier boost of good fat and protein. What's wrong with peanut butter? Besides the obvious of added sugar, hydrogenated oils and chemicals when purchased, peanuts are one of the most heavily pesticide-ridden crops and are prone to mold. Best to stay away.

2–3 SERVINGS

2 tbsp (30 ml) coconut oil

1 large yellow or white onion, sliced

Salt and black pepper, to taste

2 garlic cloves, chopped roughly

3-inch (7-cm) piece of ginger, peeled and minced

1 tbsp (7.5 g) ground coriander

2 tsp (5 g) ground cumin

½ tsp ground turmeric

1 tsp cayenne, or to taste

3 medium sweet potatoes, peeled and cut into chunks

3 ripe tomatoes, peeled and chopped (or 1 [6-oz (170-g)] can diced tomatoes)

½ cup (100 g) dry red lentils, rinsed and drained

1 tbsp (15 ml) coconut aminos

2 cups (480 ml) filtered water

4 large kale leaves, chopped into small pieces

¼ cup (45 g) natural almond butter

¼–½ cup (10–20 g) chopped fresh cilantro

Handful chopped almonds, for garnish

1 lime, optional

Heat the oil in a large pot over medium heat. Add the onion and a few pinches of salt and pepper and cook until the onion is soft, about 5 minutes. Add the garlic, ginger, coriander, cumin, turmeric and cayenne pepper. Stir and cook for 1 minute.

Mix in the sweet potatoes, tomatoes, lentils, coconut aminos and water. Bring to a boil, reduce the heat and simmer for 25 to 30 minutes, until the sweet potatoes are soft.

Stir in the kale and almond butter, and simmer on very low heat for about 5 more minutes.

Taste and adjust seasonings, adding more spice, salt and pepper to your liking.

Garnish with fresh cilantro and chopped almonds if using, and serve with lime wedges.

OMG ROASTED VEGGIE SOUP

CANCER PREVENTION · WEIGHT MANAGEMENT · SATISFYING

Comfort food at its finest. Roasting vegetables is magic—the sugars caramelize and the flavor becomes so much fuller and richer than boiling or steaming. It really makes the difference in this yummy soup.

MAKES 4 CUP-SIZE SERVINGS OR 2 LARGE BOWL SERVINGS

1 medium onion, chopped into chunks

1 medium carrot, peeled and sliced into ½-inch (13-mm) thick rounds

½ head cauliflower, cut into florets

2 cups (340 g) broccoli, cut into florets

5 red, yellow or orange organic bell peppers, cut into 1-inch (25-mm) pieces

3 cloves garlic, unpeeled

Salt and pepper, to taste

2 tbsp (3 g) dried oregano

3 tbsp (45 ml) extra virgin olive oil

3 tbsp (7.5 g) fresh basil, chopped

1 cup (240 ml) coconut milk

2 tbsp (30 ml) lemon juice

2 tbsp (18 g) nutritional yeast, optional

Preheat the oven to 400°F (204°C).

Pile the vegetables into a baking dish a few inches deep. Season with salt, pepper and oregano, then pour the olive oil over the vegetables. Mix thoroughly but gently.

Roast until tender, 30 to 40 minutes. Squeeze the soft, roasted garlic from the skins.

Transfer the vegetables to a high-speed blender (or use an immersion blender) together with the fresh basil, coconut milk, lemon juice and nutritional yeast (if using). Process until smooth. Taste and adjust seasonings as desired. Reheat in a pot if needed.

Serve hot with a drizzle of coconut milk and several drops of olive oil on top.

NORI VEGGIE BURRITO

HELPS PREVENT CANCER - STRENGTHENS BONES AND TEETH - RICH IN PROTEIN

This burrito is wrapped in a nori sheet instead of a processed-flour tortilla. Nori, a sea vegetable, provides a healthy boost of iron, protein, vitamin B$_{12}$ and iodine, keeping you nourished and glowing.

2 SERVINGS

4 nori sheets

4 tbsp (30 g) Honest Sour Cream (page 175)

¼ cup (68 g) sweet pea shoots or sprouts

¼ cup (45 g) shredded carrots

1 small cucumber, cut into matchsticks

½ avocado, sliced thinly

1 cup (200 g) black beans, drained and rinsed, divided

1 cup (245 g) "Thrive" Cheeze Sauce (page 174)

Arrange the nori sheets on a work surface with the long edges close to you. Spread the sour cream in a thin layer over the nori sheets. Layer the pea shoots, carrots, cucumber, avocado and ¼ cup (50 g) of black beans on top of the bottom one-third of the nori sheets.

Gently but firmly, roll the edge closest to you toward the center of the nori wrap, carefully creating a sushi-like roll. A bamboo sushi mat makes this easier.

With a sharp knife, carefully slice your roll in the middle and serve immediately with a side of cheeze sauce for dipping.

SAME, SAME BUT DIFFERENT THAI CURRY

PREVENTS COLON CANCER - PROMOTES WEIGHT LOSS - ENERGY BOOSTER

An awesome homemade Thai curry, made entirely from scratch—no packaged curry pastes required! This yellow curry is rich and very flavorful and makes a sumptuous dish to serve on a chilly fall or winter night. Leftovers make perfect weekday lunches.

2–3 SERVINGS

2 tbsp (30 ml) coconut oil

¼ tsp ground turmeric

1 tbsp (5 g) cumin seeds

1 large onion, sliced

3 cloves garlic, minced

3-inch (7-cm) piece of ginger, peeled and grated or minced

½ tsp ground cinnamon

½ tsp ground cardamom

¼ tsp ground cloves

¼–½ tsp cayenne pepper

¾ tsp Himalayan sea salt

2 large carrots, peeled and sliced

2 medium sweet potatoes, peeled and cubed

1 (13.5-oz [382-g]) can coconut milk

1 cup (240 ml) water

1 cup (152 g) fresh or frozen green peas

1 organic red bell pepper, seeded and chopped

⅓ cup (60 g) tahini

1 tbsp (15 ml) maple syrup (or stevia, to taste)

Heat the oil in large skillet over medium heat. Add the turmeric and cumin seeds and cook until the seeds sizzle, about 30 seconds.

Add the onion and cook until caramelized, about 5 minutes, stirring occasionally. Add the garlic and ginger and cook another 2 to 3 minutes, stirring occasionally. Add the cinnamon, cardamom, cloves, cayenne, salt, carrots, potatoes, coconut milk and water. Reduce heat to low and simmer for 15 minutes, covered.

Add the peas and red pepper. Continue to simmer, covered, for an additional 10 minutes or until the vegetables are tender. Remove from the heat and stir in the tahini and maple syrup.

Serve with Basic Green Salad (page 91), or on a bed of wild rice.

KITCHARI

CLEANSING · LOWERS CHOLESTEROL · PROTEIN PACKED

Try our easy recipe for the Ayurvedic dish kitchari to purify digestion and cleanse systemic toxins. Think of it as a vegetarian, Indian version of American chili. Unlike chili, it's cleansing, easy to digest and provides complete proteins, entirely plant-based. You'll be surprised how warming and comforting it is!

3–4 SERVINGS

½ cup (105 g) basmati rice

1 cup (200 g) mung dal (split yellow lentils)

6 cups (1.4 L) filtered water

1 cup (180 g) chopped organic carrots

½ cup (75 g) organic frozen peas (or any other vegetables of your choice)

½ tsp mustard seeds

2 tbsp (30 ml) coconut oil

1-inch (25-mm) piece of ginger root, grated

½ tsp ground coriander

½ tsp ground cumin

½ tsp whole cumin seeds

½ tsp ground turmeric

1 pinch hing, optional

½ tsp sea salt

½ cup (20 g) chopped fresh cilantro, for garnish

Soak the rice and mung dal in a large pot for a few hours, rinsing every so often.

Rinse and wash the rice and dal and place back into the pot. Add the water to the pot and cook covered until they become soft, about 20 minutes.

While that is cooking, prepare any vegetables you wish to add. We like carrots and peas, but feel free to explore other vegetables like spinach, celery, kale and bok choy as well. Cut them into small pieces. Add the vegetables to the cooked rice and dal mixture and cook 10 minutes longer.

In a separate saucepan, sauté the mustard seeds in the coconut oil until they pop. Add the other spices and mix together to release the flavors. Stir the sautéed spices into the cooked dal, rice and vegetable mixture.

Add the sea salt and serve by topping with fresh cilantro.

MAMMA J'S LAZY CABBAGE "ROLLS"

WEIGHT LOSS - HEALTHY SKIN AND HAIR - CANCER PREVENTION

If you like cabbage rolls, you'll love this dish. An alternative to wrapping cabbage rolls and just as tasty. This is a meat-free version of the classic inspired by Nikki's mom.

2–3 SERVINGS

1 tbsp (15 ml) coconut oil

1 medium onion, chopped

2 large carrots, diced

2 cloves garlic, minced

2 tsp (1 g) dried or fresh oregano

Pinch of thyme

1 tsp salt

1 tsp pepper

5 large tomatoes, diced

1 (8-oz [227-g]) can no-sugar-added tomato paste

½ lemon, juiced

1 tbsp (15 ml) molasses

1 cup (240 ml) filtered water

1 small head cabbage, chopped

1 cup (200 g) yellow split peas, soaked and drained

½ cup (105 g) uncooked brown rice, soaked and drained

In a deep-dish skillet, warm the coconut oil over medium-low heat. Add the onion, carrots and garlic, and cook for 5 minutes, or until softened. Stir in the dried herbs, salt, pepper, diced tomatoes, tomato paste, lemon juice, molasses and water, then bring to a low boil.

Mix in the chopped cabbage, and stir to combine all ingredients. Reduce to a simmer and cook for 10 minutes.

Stir in the split peas and brown rice. Cover and cook over low-medium heat for approximately 30 to 35 minutes or until cooked and thickened. Enjoy!

EASY SLOW COOKER CHICKPEA RATATOUILLE

BONE HEALTH · WEIGHT LOSS · PROTEIN PACKED

This dish is ridiculously easy to make, loaded with vegetables and protein-rich chickpeas. Serve alongside a Basic Green Salad (page 91), over brown or wild rice, or my favorite, zucchini noodles!

3–4 SERVINGS

1 large eggplant, peeled and cut into 1-inch (25-mm) cubes

½ winter squash or 2 yams, peeled and chopped into cubes

3 medium tomatoes, chopped

3 medium zucchini, cubed

2 medium carrots, peeled and chopped

2 medium onions, chopped

1 large red bell pepper, chopped

1 large yellow bell pepper, chopped

1 (15-oz [425-g]) can of chickpeas, drained and rinsed, or 1½ cups (227 g) cooked chickpeas

2 tbsp (30 ml) coconut oil

2 (6-oz [170-g]) cans tomato paste

2 tbsp (30 ml) balsamic vinegar

½ cup (20 g) minced fresh basil

2 cloves garlic, minced

½ tsp dried oregano

½ tsp dried thyme, optional

2 bay leaves, optional

Sea salt and pepper, to taste

½ cup (90 g) pitted ripe olives, drained and chopped

Place the vegetables and chickpeas in a 5-quart (5-L) slow cooker coated with coconut oil.

Stir in the tomato paste, balsamic vinegar, basil, garlic, oregano, thyme, bay leaves and sea salt and pepper. Cover and cook on high for 3 to 4 hours or until the vegetables are tender.

Add in the olives and cook for another 5 to 10 minutes. Serve over whole-grain rice or zucchini noodles.

JUST THE PORTOBELLO BURGER

HELPS KEEP YOU HYDRATED - SOURCE OF B VITAMINS - FULL OF MINERALS

Are you looking to spice up your grilling game? What better option than portobello mushroom burgers to eat on a gorgeous summer night? We chose to get a little creative with this recipe by excluding the bun and making the dish completely gluten-free and all veggies! This is a great recipe to impress company—simple and very few ingredients that create a beautiful dish.

2 SERVINGS

2 large portobello mushroom caps

3 tbsp (45 ml) balsamic vinegar

1 tbsp (15 ml) coconut aminos

1 tbsp (15 ml) organic Dijon mustard

1 tsp fresh minced garlic

2 tsp (1 g) dried basil

1 tsp dried oregano

½ tsp ground black pepper

Coconut oil

1 large tomato, sliced

1 avocado, sliced

1 cup (270 g) pea shoots (sprouts)

Remove the mushroom stems. Trim about ½-inch (13-mm) off of the mushroom top (as if slicing a bun). Combine the balsamic, coconut aminos, Dijon mustard, garlic, basil, oregano and pepper in a small bowl and mix well.

Place the mushroom caps on a cookie sheet covered with foil and add a little coconut oil to prevent sticking.

Pour the marinade over each mushroom cap with a large spoon, flip and repeat. Let sit for about 10 minutes.

Preheat the grill or oven to 425°F (218°C).

Grill or bake the mushrooms for about 10 minutes. Check and see if they are done; otherwise, flip them and continue cooking for another 10 minutes.

Place the bottom of the mushroom cap on a plate—add your choice of toppings and top with the other half of the mushroom cap.

WALNUT FLAX BURGER

HEALTHY HAIR AND SKIN · WEIGHT LOSS · RICH IN OMEGA-3 FATTY ACIDS

If you're in the mood for a healthy, wholesome, raw twist on the average burger, look no further. This is by far my favorite plant-based burger made from simple, unprocessed and whole-food ingredients. The best part—it is all assembled in a food processor or blender in a matter of, oh, 3 minutes, and doesn't even need to be cooked afterward!

2 SERVINGS

1 cup (116 g) raw walnuts, soaked

½ cup (80 g) flaxseeds

1 cup (54 g) sun-dried tomatoes

¼ cup (10 g) fresh basil

2 tbsp (30 ml) apple cider vinegar

Sea salt to taste

Coconut oil, optional

Process all of the burger ingredients except the coconut oil in a food processor until well blended. Do not overprocess. It's nice to leave a few chunks here and there for some texture.

Form the dough into 2 patties.

Personally, I love them raw, but if you prefer to cook them, lightly cover a small baking pan with coconut oil and bake at 300°F (149°C) for 30 to 35 minutes, flipping once.

Serve on a sprouted-grain bun with lettuce, tomato, avocado, sprouts and Homemade Ketchup (page 171) or on top of the Basic Green Salad (page 91) with Sun-Dried Tomato Basil Marinara Sauce (page 171).

CURRY FALAFEL BURGER

HEALTHY DIGESTION - SUPPORTS WEIGHT LOSS - PROTEIN-RICH

These burgers are a perfect combination of chickpeas mixed with spices and herbs and a hint of lemon zest. Unlike normal falafel, which is deep-fried, these guys are baked, making them an insanely healthy and satisfying choice.

4 SERVINGS

1½ tbsp (22 ml) olive or coconut oil, plus more for greasing

1 cup (40 g) fresh cilantro

1 cup (40 g) fresh parsley

1–2 cloves garlic

1 (15-oz [425-g]) can or 2 cups (400 g) cooked chickpeas, drained and dried

½ avocado, mashed

1 tbsp (7 g) curry powder

½ organic lemon, juice and zest

1 tsp salt

1–2 tbsp (8–16 g) chickpea flour (sub a gluten-free flour if needed)

Preheat the oven to 425°F (218°C), line a baking sheet with parchment paper then lightly coat the parchment with olive oil.

Place the cilantro, parsley and garlic into a food processor then pulse until finely chopped but not liquefied. Add the chickpeas and avocado, then pulse until the beans are chopped small but still have texture. Be careful not to overwork and avoid turning it into a purée.

Transfer the mixture to a medium mixing bowl then add the curry powder, lemon juice, lemon zest, olive oil and salt. Stir until well combined, then add 1 tablespoon (8 g) of chickpea flour and stir once again until the ingredients are well combined. The mixture should hold together when compressed. Add a bit more flour if needed to bind the mixture.

With your hands, form the patties to the desired size and place each one on the prepared baking sheet. Bake for 10 minutes, then carefully turn over the falafel and bake another 10 to 13 minutes, until browned nicely on both sides.

Remove from the oven and let cool for 5 minutes before serving. Serve with Basic Green Salad (page 91), fresh tomatoes and Miso Ginger Dressing (page 170).

LOADED BAKED YAM WITH MISO GINGER DRESSING

BOOSTS IMMUNITY - CONTROLS BLOOD SUGAR - ANTIAGING

Loaded with zesty black bean salsa and topped with creamy vegan sour cream, this baked yam will quickly become one of your favorites. One large yam contains around 30 percent of the daily recommended values of vitamin C and can help protect the body from disease and cell damage. They can also help reduce inflammation throughout the body. Because of this, yams are a good option for athletes or those who suffer from chronic illnesses such as cystitis or arthritis.

2 SERVINGS

2 yams

1 cup (200 g) Black Bean & Pineapple Salsa (page 175)

½ cup (120 ml) Miso Ginger Dressing (page 170), divided

Sea salt and fresh ground pepper, to taste

10 cherry tomatoes

½ avocado, diced

½ cup (20 g) fresh cilantro, chopped

Preheat the oven to 400°F (204°C). Wash the yams and pierce with a fork several times. Place them on a cookie sheet and bake for about 1 hour or until tender.

While the yams are baking, prepare the salsa and the dressing. Set aside.

Remove the yams from the oven, then cut them open and mash each side with a fork. Sprinkle on a little sea salt and pepper.

Load on the toppings: start with the bean salsa, tomatoes, avocado and cilantro. Drizzle ¼ cup (60 ml) of dressing over each potato. Serve immediately.

GREEN COLLARD WRAPS WITH NUTTY LIME CARROT SALAD

LOWERS RISK OF CANCER - RICH IN VITAMINS AND MINERALS - FIGHTS DEPRESSION

These vibrant, raw veggie wraps are bursting with numerous whole foods. Inspired by nature, we assembled a rainbow of vegetables and stuffed them into another awesome vegetable: the collard. This dark leafy green is high in vitamins A, C and K, which means it's an excellent source of antioxidants and anti-inflammatory nutrients. Collards are not only super nutritious, they also happen to be the world's healthiest sandwich wraps. They're gluten-free, completely unprocessed and are super low in calories!

2 SERVINGS

2 collard greens

½ cup (120 ml) Nutty Lime Carrot Salad (page 91), divided

½ avocado, sliced

Sprouts or micro greens

Raisin Chutney (page 170), optional

Wash and dry the collard greens, and then use a paring knife to shave down the stems. This will make them much easier to fold and eat.

Place the collard greens on a flat surface and spread ¼ cup (58 g) of carrot salad near the top/middle of each leaf. Fill each leaf with the avocado slices and sprouts, splitting each amount between the two wraps. Wrap the leaves as you would a burrito. Cut each wrap in half and enjoy.

Serve with Raisin Chutney on the side if desired.

NOTE: **The collard leaf wrapping technique can be a little finicky, so we put together a quick how-to video available on www.activevegetarian.com. With a couple of practice runs, you'll be a pro in no time!**

SNACK TIME

Snacks are essential for making sure we get the proper amount of nutrients. They refuel our bodies and allow us to be productive at work and school and during fitness activities. The challenge is to find a snack that isn't processed, boxed or full of genetically modified organisms (GMOs). The following collection of snacks are good for you, portable, appealing, inexpensive and easy to make.

SWEET BAKED ORANGE PLANTAINS

IMMUNE SYSTEM BOOSTER - HIGH IN VITAMIN C - DIGESTIVE SUPPORT

Baked plantains make a decadent, no-sugar-added treat to satisfy your sweet tooth. They taste like candy! Choose really ripe plantains. If they're black, that's totally okay as long as the inside isn't super mushy or moldy.

2 SERVINGS

2 plantains, very ripe

1 tsp coconut oil

2 small or 1 large orange, juiced (about ½ cup [120 ml])

1 tbsp (15 ml) maple syrup or molasses

1 tsp ground cinnamon

Preheat the oven to 350°F (177°C). Lightly coat a baking dish with coconut oil. Peel each plantain and cut into 2-inch (5-cm) chunks. Place the plantain pieces in the prepared baking pan.

Pour the orange juice into a mixing bowl, then add in the maple syrup or molasses and cinnamon. Whisk well. Pour the mixture evenly over the plantain pieces. Bake for 30 to 35 minutes, or until tender, turning once or twice. Serve warm or cold as a snack.

LEMON PEPPER ROASTED CHICKPEAS

PROTEIN PACKED - BLOOD SUGAR STABILIZER - PROMOTES INTESTINAL HEALTH

Enter crunchy roasted chickpeas. These are addictive little snacks, crunchy and flavorful but actually good for you too! Eat them alone or use them as a topping for salads and soups.

2–3 SERVINGS

1 (15-oz [425-g]) can chickpeas, about 2 cups (400 g) cooked

2 tbsp (30 ml) extra virgin olive oil

1 organic lemon, juiced and zested

½ tsp Himalayan salt

½ tsp ground black pepper

1 tsp maple syrup

Preheat the oven to 400°F (204°C). Using a strainer, drain and rinse the chickpeas well. Drain thoroughly, then set chickpeas on a paper towel to absorb any remaining liquid.

Place the fully dry chickpeas into a deep bowl. Mix together the olive oil, lemon juice, zest, salt, black pepper and maple syrup. Pour over the chickpeas and toss until they are all evenly coated.

Put the chickpeas on a dry baking sheet. Roast the chickpeas in the oven for about 40 minutes, shaking the pan every 10 minutes or so to let the chickpeas cook evenly, careful not to burn. Remove the pan from the oven and let the chickpeas cool on the baking sheet. Taste and salt again if necessary. Serve warm or at room temperature as a snack or as an addition to your wraps, soups and salads.

FIVE-INGREDIENT PROTEIN BARS

GREAT SOURCE OF ENERGY - PROMOTES HEALTHY DIGESTION - HELPS WEIGHT LOSS

You only need five ingredients and a few minutes to whip up these healthy protein bars. Perfect for snacking or after a workout!

MAKES 9 BARS

1½ cups (174 g) walnuts

2 tbsp (23 g) plant-based protein powder (we prefer Garden of Life, chocolate cacao)

⅓ cup (60 g) mixed seeds (flax, sunflower, pumpkin, hemp, cacao nibs)

2 plantains, cut into chunks

3 tbsp (50 g) extra-dark chocolate

Preheat the oven to 325°F (163°C).

Lightly grease a small baking dish with coconut oil. Chop the walnuts in a food processor until a fine consistency is reached. Do not overprocess; keep some larger pieces. Place this walnut meal into a large bowl and add in the protein powder and seeds. Mix well.

Place the peeled plantains into the food processor and blend until liquefied. Stir the plantains into the dry ingredients until incorporated and a dough is formed.

Transfer the dough into the prepared baking dish. Distribute it evenly, pressing down using a spatula or wet hands. Bake for 12 to 15 minutes.

Remove the bars from the oven and let cool completely before slicing.

While the bars are cooling, melt the dark chocolate in a saucepan over medium heat. Mix frequently until the chocolate is fully melted. Remove from heat. Using your hands, dip each bar into the melted chocolate to coat about half of each bar. Set the bars on parchment paper to cool and add an additional sprinkle of seeds if desired.

Bars can be stored at room temperature for up to 1 week or refrigerated for up to a month.

NO BAKE FIG CRUMB BARS

POWERFUL ANTIOXIDANT - RICH SOURCE OF IRON - STRENGTHENS BONES

Figs, rich in antioxidants, are combined with fiber-filled oats and maple syrup to make a snack that is healthier than a standard cookie or energy bar. They're the perfect snack to keep with you throughout the day to eat when you're feeling hungry or need a burst of energy.

MAKES 12 BARS

DOUGH

1 cup (80 g) old-fashioned oats

½ cup (38 g) unsweetened shredded coconut

2 tbsp (30 ml) coconut oil

4 tbsp (60 ml) maple syrup

1 tsp vanilla

Pinch of sea salt

FILLING

10 dried figs

4 dates, pitted

2 tbsp (30 ml) hot water

2 tbsp (30 ml) lemon juice

½ tsp ground cinnamon

¼ tsp ground ginger

TOPPING

½ cup (40 g) old-fashioned oats

3 dates, pitted

1 tbsp (15 ml) maple syrup

½ tsp ground cinnamon

¼ tsp ground cardamom, optional

Line a small pan with parchment paper.

In a food processor, pulse the oats until they're broken down into a flour-like consistency. Add in the coconut, coconut oil, maple syrup, vanilla and sea salt, and process until a sticky ball of dough forms.

Transfer the dough to the pan and press down evenly with your hands. Place in the refrigerator or freezer while you make the fig filling.

For the filling, snip off the fig stems, and put the figs, dates and hot water into the food processor. Grind to a coarse paste. Stir in the remaining filling ingredients and process again. Stop and scrape down the sides as needed. It should be a sticky paste-like consistency. Scoop out the fig filling and spread it evenly on top of the crust, using a wet spatula. Place back in the refrigerator or freezer.

For the topping, add the oats and dates to a food processor. Pulse until just combined. Add in the maple syrup, cinnamon and cardamom (if using) and pulse a few times until you get a crumbly mixture. Be careful not to process too much.

Sprinkle the topping evenly on top of the fig layer. Press it down gently with your hands. Place back in the freezer for 1 hour to set.

Cut into 12 bars and serve chilled!

CARDAMOM GINGER BLISS BALLS

POWERFUL ANTIOXIDANT - RICH SOURCE OF IRON - STRENGTHENS BONES

Bliss balls are so easy to make: there's no cooking and no lengthy preparation required. They're made with dried fruits, nuts, pure cacao, spices and a generous amount of fresh ginger to give you a taste of heaven. Enjoy one or two satisfying, guilt-free treats during midday slumps, after yoga or whenever you crave some bliss.

MAKES 14 MEDIUM BLISS BALLS

14 dates, pitted

½ lemon, juiced

1 cup (116 g) raw cashews (soaked overnight and drained)

½ cup (58 g) pecans (soaked overnight and drained)

3 tbsp (21 g) cocoa powder

2 tbsp (23 g) cacao nibs (optional, gives it a nice crunch)

1 tbsp (15 g) fresh ginger, grated

1 tsp ground cardamom

Place the dates in a food processor together with the lemon juice and process until you achieve a creamy texture. Add the remaining ingredients and process until they are combined but the dough is still chunky and sticky.

Scoop 1 to 1½ tablespoons (15 to 22 g) of the dough and roll it in your hand. Repeat until you have rolled all of the dough.

Store in the refrigerator for up to 7 days or in the freezer for a couple of weeks.

NOTE: **If you want to get fancy, roll the balls in toppings such as cocoa powder, hemp seeds, shredded coconut, etc.**

SALT & VINEGAR ROASTED SQUASH

PROTEIN PACKED - BLOOD SUGAR STABILIZER - PROMOTES INTESTINAL HEALTH

Roasted Japanese squash is not only a great snack, it also works as a light side dish. We enjoy it straight from the oven or cold—or if we end up with leftovers, we add it to a salad for lunch the following day.

4 SERVINGS

1 large kabocha squash, peeled, seeded and cut into 1-inch (25-mm) cubes

2 tbsp (30 ml) olive oil

2 tbsp (30 ml) maple syrup

2 tbsp (30 ml) apple cider vinegar

1 tsp ground cinnamon

1 tsp ground cumin

1 tsp sea salt

Dash cayenne, optional

Preheat the oven to 425°F (218°C) and line a large baking sheet with parchment paper.

Toss the squash cubes with olive oil, place them on the prepared baking sheet and bake for 35 to 45 minutes, turning once and rotating the pan once, until the edges are lightly browned and the centers are tender. Since oven temperatures vary, check the squash every so often to make sure it is not roasting quicker than expected.

While the squash is roasting, mix the maple syrup, apple cider vinegar, cinnamon, cumin, sea salt and optional cayenne in a small bowl to create a dressing.

Once the squash is done baking, remove it from the oven. Pour the dressing over the squash, coating every piece, and serve.

SO EASY SEEDY CRACKERS

PROTEIN-RICH · GRAIN-FREE · HORMONAL SUPPORT

These are made with just a few simple ingredients and are the perfect homemade cracker. They're always good to have on hand as they go well with dips, spreads, veggies—and are also wonderful on their own!

MAKES 20–24 CRACKERS

2 cups (240 g) mixed seeds (sunflower, flax, chia, pumpkin, hemp, black and white sesame seeds)

1 cup (240 ml) filtered water

1 tbsp (15 ml) maple syrup

½ tbsp (2 g) kelp flakes (optional but recommended)

1 tbsp (8 g) spices of your choice (pepper, garlic, curry, onion, chili and cayenne all work well)

Place all of the seeds in a fine-mesh strainer and rinse them well. Transfer the seeds to a mixing bowl and combine well with the water. Let it sit for at least 30 minutes or overnight.

Preheat the oven to 350°F (177°C). Line a baking sheet with parchment paper.

After soaking the seeds, mix in the maple syrup, kelp and chosen spices. Using a wet spatula, flatten the seed mixture onto the prepared baking sheet (to about ¼-inch [6-mm] thick).

Bake for 20 minutes. Remove the cookie sheet from the oven, flip the whole cracker over and remove the baking paper. Don't worry if some parts of the cracker break off. Return to the oven to bake for another 10 minutes, until fully dry, crisp and golden around the edges. Check often to ensure it does not burn.

As soon as you remove the crackers from the oven, use either a pizza cutter or knife and cut the crackers into squares.

If you prefer crunchy crackers, place them back in the warm oven with the heat off for an additional 8 to 10 minutes.

Allow the crackers to cool and crisp up a little more and serve with hummus, veggies or dips or as a crunchy salad topping.

Store in an airtight container for up to 3 weeks.

INDULGENCES

Living a healthy vegan lifestyle doesn't mean that you can't enjoy the phenomenal flavors of your favorite treats every once in a while. Learn just how easy it is to enjoy your favorite homespun goodies without compromising your health or values. Some of these recipes are quite rich and are intended as a whole-food treat for special occasions, especially if you are trying to lose weight, maintain weight loss or deal with a health condition.

ONE-INGREDIENT HEALTHY ICE CREAM, AKA NICECREAM

ENERGY FOR ATHLETES - BONE HEALTH - MOOD ENHANCER

Using bananas as the base, you simply cut and chill, then add your favorite healthy toppings. There you have it, your very own healthy treat! Keep some peeled bananas In your freezer so they'll be ready whenever you are.

2 SERVINGS

3 ripe bananas

Peel the bananas and cut them into even slices. Place the slices in a glass bowl and freeze overnight.

Place the frozen banana slices in a high-speed blender or food processor and process until smooth. Scrape down the sides occasionally and continue to blend until smooth, approximately 3 to 5 minutes. Be careful, however, not to over-process, as the ice cream will become too liquid.

Scoop into two bowls and enjoy immediately as a soft serve. For firmer ice cream, place in an airtight, freezer-safe container and freeze for at least 1 hour.

OPTIONAL: Garnish with your favorite wholesome toppings, such as sliced fresh fruit, coconut flakes, cacao nibs, granola and raisins.

NOTE: Once you have the basic Nicecream down, it's time to go ahead and get creative with other ingredients. Try adding different fruits for a new flavor combination—berries and mango are our personal favorite. You could also add carob or cacao for a chocolate twist, or vanilla bean for a classic vanilla ice cream vibe.

MO' MANGO NICECREAM

Healthy enough to eat for breakfast, this mango Nicecream is so creamy, rich and smooth. All the qualities of real ice cream with none of the guilt!

2 SERVINGS

2 ripe bananas, peeled, sliced and frozen

1 cup (180 g) mango chunks, frozen

1 organic lime, zested

Place the frozen banana slices, frozen mango and lime zest in the high-speed blender or food processor and process until smooth. Occasionally scrape down the sides and continue to blend until smooth, approximately 3 to 5 minutes. Be careful, however, not to over-process, as the ice cream will become too liquid.

Serve immediately or for firmer ice cream, place in an airtight, freezer-safe container and freeze for at least 1 hour or until solid.

MOUTHWATERING MOLASSES

MOOD ENHANCING · POWERS THE BRAIN · PROMOTES HEALTHY SKIN

This Mouthwatering Molasses Nicecream is naturally sweet, filling and nutrient-dense! Blackstrap molasses is high in nutrients like calcium and iron and makes a great addition to any plant-based diet.

2 SERVINGS

3 tbsp (28 g) raisins

2 ripe bananas, peeled, sliced and frozen

1 tbsp (22 g) blackstrap molasses

1 tsp ground cinnamon

Soak the raisins in hot water for at least 5 minutes. Place the frozen banana slices, molasses and cinnamon in a high-speed blender or food processor and process until smooth. Occasionally scrape down the sides and continue to blend until smooth, approximately 3 to 5 minutes. Be careful, however, not to over-process, as the ice cream will become too liquid.

Drain the raisins well and pat dry with a paper towel. Gently mix into the ice cream by hand. Serve immediately or for firmer ice cream, place in an airtight, freezer-safe container and freeze for at least 1 hour or until solid.

VERY BERRY BLAST

MUSCLE-BUILDING · PROMOTES DIGESTION · ANTIOXIDANT

A protein-packed, healthy yet equally tasty berry Nicecream with a hint of vanilla is a refreshing and nutritious way to treat yourself!

2 SERVINGS

2 ripe bananas, peeled, sliced and frozen

1 cup (150 g) frozen berries (blueberries, raspberries and strawberries)

1 scoop vanilla protein powder (We prefer RAW Organic Protein by Garden of Life)

Place the frozen banana slices and frozen berries in a high-speed blender or food processor and process until smooth. Occasionally scrape down the sides and continue to blend until smooth, approximately 3 to 5 minutes. Be careful, however, not to over-process, as the ice cream will become too liquid.

Add the protein powder and mix for few more seconds or until well combined.

Serve immediately, or for firmer ice cream, place in an airtight, freezer-safe container and freeze for at least 1 hour or until solid.

CHEEKY MONKEY

MOOD ENHANCING · POWERS THE BRAIN · PROMOTES HEALTHY SKIN

This just might be the best chocolate ice cream you've ever had! Who knew that bananas could create such magic?

2 SERVINGS

2 ripe bananas, peeled, sliced and frozen

3 tbsp (21 g) unsweetened cacao powder

2 tbsp (30 ml) maple syrup

2 tbsp (15 g) raw unsalted walnuts, chopped

¼ cup (25 g) extra-dark chocolate bar, chopped into tiny pieces

Place the frozen banana slices, cacao powder and maple syrup in a high-speed blender or food processor and process until smooth. Occasionally scrape down the sides and continue to blend until smooth, approximately 3 to 5 minutes. Be careful, however, not to over-process, as the ice cream will become too liquid.

Add in the walnuts and chocolate pieces and blend for a few more seconds.

Serve immediately, or for firmer ice cream, place in an airtight, freezer-safe container and freeze for at least 1 hour or until solid.

RAW NANAIMO BARS

HEALTHY TREAT - CURBS SWEET CRAVINGS - SUPPORTS CARDIOVASCULAR HEALTH

As we are two proud Canadians, this dessert spread wouldn't be complete without Nanaimo bars. Layers of chewy coconut, creamy custard and sweet chocolate come together in this classic BC treat that's truly a fan favorite from coast to coast. We gave this famed Canadian dessert, traditionally made with loads of butter and sugar, a healthy vegan makeover.

MAKES 12 BARS

BOTTOM LAYER

1 cup (75 g) shredded coconut

½ cup (75 g) dates

½ cup (50 g) dry cranberries

½ cup (85 g) almonds, soaked for 12 hours or overnight

¼ cup (28 g) raw cacao powder, unsweetened

MIDDLE LAYER

2 cups (222 g) raw cashews, soaked 4 to 6 hours or overnight

¼ cup (60 ml) maple syrup

2 tbsp (30 ml) melted coconut oil

4 tbsp (60 ml) lemon juice

2 tsp (10 ml) pure vanilla extract

TOP LAYER

1 (100 g) 80-85 percent dark vegan chocolate bar (preferably raw)

2 tbsp (28 g) coconut oil

3 tbsp (34 g) cacao nibs

For the bottom layer, coat a small square cake pan with coconut oil or line it with parchment paper.

Add all of the bottom layer ingredients to a food processor fitted with the S blade. Process until the mixture is broken down and begins to stick together. Scrape down the sides of the food processor as needed.

Press the crust into the bottom of your prepared pan using a spatula. Place the dish in the refrigerator.

For the middle layer, rinse the soaked cashews and blend all of the middle layer ingredients in a clean food processor until you have a smooth cream filling, about 8 to 10 minutes. Spread the cream evenly on the top of the base and put the dish back into the refrigerator.

For the top layer, place the vegan dark chocolate and coconut oil in a small pot and melt over low heat. Make sure you keep mixing as it melts so it doesn't burn.

Pour the chocolate layer over the middle layer and finally, sprinkle with cacao nibs.

Return the pan to the refrigerator. Allow the chocolate and the bars to firm up for about 3 hours or overnight before slicing.

Keep bars in the refrigerator for 3 to 5 days.

NOTE: These are very rich; eat in moderation!

EPIC BROWNIES

HEALTHY TREAT - IMPROVES MOOD - GREAT SOURCE OF MAGNESIUM

We swapped butter with avocado and created these healthier brownies that are super fudgy and still delicious. You seriously need to try this recipe full of wholesome ingredients.

MAKES 9 BROWNIES

¼ cup (55 g) coconut oil, plus more for greasing

1 cup (100 g) chopped vegan dark chocolate (minimum 80 percent cacao)

1 large ripe avocado, about 1 cup (230 g) mashed

½ cup (120 ml) maple syrup

2 tsp (10 ml) vanilla

2 flax "eggs" (1 tbsp [7.5 g] ground flax meal and 3 tbsp [45 ml] water per "egg," whisked for 5 minutes)

1 cup (96 g) almond flour

¼ cup (28 g) raw cacao powder, unsweetened

¼ tsp sea salt

Preheat the oven to 350°F (177°C). Grease an 8 x 8-inch (20 x 20-cm) cake pan with coconut oil.

Using a saucepan over medium heat, melt the coconut oil. Turn the heat off and add pieces of dark chocolate. Mix frequently until the chocolate is fully melted and ingredients are well combined. Set the mixture aside and let it cool.

In a food processor, process the avocado, maple syrup, vanilla and flax "eggs" until well combined. Add the almond flour, cacao powder and sea salt to the food processor and mix for another minute on low.

After the chocolate mixture has cooled in the pot, about 4 to 5 minutes, add it to the food processor and mix one more time until everything is well combined. Pour the batter into the prepared cake pan.

Bake for about 30 minutes or until a toothpick inserted into the center of the brownies comes out clean, but still moist. Cool the brownies completely before cutting. They will keep in an airtight container for 3 days.

NOTE: **You can make your own almond flour by grinding whole almonds in a high-speed blender or food processor.**

BABOVKA - GINGER PEAR CAKE WITH SALTED CARAMEL SAUCE

GREAT SOURCE OF IRON · DIABETES-FRIENDLY SWEETENER · PROMOTES BONE HEALTH

Growing up in the Czech Republic, it was a tradition to finish our weekend lunch with something sweet. Babovka, or Bundt cake, is an undisputed Sunday classic. This cake has a very rich molasses flavor and a nice punch of spicy ginger.

12 SERVINGS

1 cup (85 g) walnut flour (finely ground walnuts)

2 cups (260 g) spelt flour

⅓ cup (38 g) walnut pieces

⅓ cup (63 g) raw coconut sugar

1½ tsp (6 g) baking soda

1 tbsp (7.5 g) ground ginger

1 tbsp (7.5 g) ground nutmeg

¼ tsp sea salt

4 tbsp (60 ml) melted coconut oil

1 cup (240 ml) warm water

3 tbsp (45 ml) maple syrup

½ cup (175 g) blackstrap molasses

½ lemon, juiced

¼ cup (60 ml) Basic Almond Milk (page 71)

1 tsp natural vanilla extract

3 small organic pears, peeled and cut into ½-inch (13-mm) dices

SALTED CARAMEL SAUCE

1 cup (152 g) pitted dates (soaked)

¼ cup (60 ml) Basic Almond Milk (page 71)

¾ tsp sea salt (or to taste)

Preheat the oven to 350°F (177°C) and grease a Bundt pan with a little coconut oil and set aside.

Place the walnut flour in a large bowl along with the spelt flour, walnut pieces, coconut sugar, baking soda, ginger, nutmeg and salt.

In a medium bowl, whisk together the melted coconut oil, water, maple syrup, molasses, lemon juice, almond milk and vanilla.

Mix together the liquid and dry ingredients slowly. Once there are no chunks, fold in the pears and pour the mixture into the prepared Bundt pan.

Bake for 55 to 65 minutes, until cooked through. Use a toothpick to make sure it is fully cooked.

Let cool for 5 minutes then use a knife to carefully loosen any stuck edges. Invert the cake over a wire rack and lift off the pan. Let the cake cool completely.

Mix all of the ingredients for the salted caramel sauce in a high-speed blender. Blend until the sauce can drizzle off a spoon easily, adding more nut milk if needed.

Pour the caramel sauce over the cake, and garnish with extra chopped walnuts if desired. Store the cake in the refrigerator for up to 3 days.

NO BAKE KEY LIME "CHEESECAKE"

RICH AND CREAMY · SERIOUSLY AMAZING · HIGH IN IRON

This raw dessert tastes like a lighter version of a key lime pie. The combination of lime and vanilla sync perfectly together and give this vegan cheesecake a smooth and slightly tangy taste. It's not too sweet, with the crust adding a delicious crunchy texture.

12 SERVINGS

CRUST

2 cups (232 g) mixed raw nuts and seeds of your choice (we use a mix of cashews, pistachios, pumpkin seeds and shredded coconut)

4 large Medjool dates (or 6 small dates)

1 lime, juiced

2 tbsp (28 g) coconut oil, softened

Dash of sea salt

FILLING

1½ cups (167 g) cashews, soaked (for 8 hours or overnight)

2 tbsp (30 ml) melted coconut oil

2 tbsp (30 ml) maple syrup

½ cup (120 ml) full-fat coconut milk

1 vanilla bean or 2 tsp (10 ml) vanilla extract

1½ limes, juiced

Zest of 1 organic lime plus 1 tbsp (10 g) for garnish

½ tsp spirulina powder (feel free to add more for extra nutrients and richer color)

Place all of the crust ingredients in a food processor and process into a fine crumble. Scoop this mixture into a spring form pan or pie dish and press it down with your fingers to form a thin crust. Place in the freezer while working on the filling.

For the filling, rinse the cashews and place them in a food processor along with the coconut oil, maple syrup, coconut milk and vanilla. Blend well until the mixture is smooth and creamy, scraping down the sides as needed.

Pour half of the mixture onto the base, and spread evenly. With the remaining mixture, add the lime juice, lime zest and spirulina powder and blend. Carefully pour this mixture onto the base, spread evenly and sprinkle with lime zest.

Store in the freezer for at least 6 to 8 hours and remove when firmly set. After it is frozen, you can refrigerate it and it will be ready to serve within about 1 hour. The cheesecake can be stored in the freezer for a week.

DUTCH APPLE CRUMBLE PIE

ANTIOXIDANT - HEART HEALTH - HELPS CONTROL APPETITE

Everything about this dessert makes it the top request for family gatherings and one of our favorite apple pie recipes. Try a warm slice with a scoop of plain Nicecream (page 151), dusted lightly with ground cinnamon. Or just have it plain, and allow the crunchy crumble topping to have its moment.

6 SERVINGS

1 cup (96 g) oat flour (see note)

1 cup (75 g) shredded coconut

½ cup (120 ml) maple syrup

½ cup (40 g) old-fashioned oats

¼ cup (55 g) coconut oil, softened

2 heaping tsp (5 g) ground cinnamon

FILLING

4–6 large apples, peeled and chopped

2 tbsp (30 ml) lemon juice

1 tsp pure vanilla extract

1–2 tsp ground cinnamon or apple pie spice

1¼ cups (300 ml) filtered water

2 tbsp (30 ml) maple syrup

4 tbsp (43 g) flax meal or ground flaxseed

Preheat the oven to 350°F (177°C).

In a large bowl, combine the crust ingredients; set aside 1 cup (170 g) for the topping. Press remaining crumb mixture into an ungreased 9-inch (23-cm) pie plate; set aside.

For the filling, place the apple slices in a large bowl. Toss with the lemon juice, vanilla and cinnamon.

In a medium saucepan, combine the water, maple syrup and flax meal or ground flaxseed until smooth; bring to a boil. Cook and stir for 2 minutes until thickened. Remove from the heat and mix in the apples to combine.

Pour the filling over the crust and top evenly with the reserved crumb mixture. Bake for 40 to 45 minutes or until crust is golden brown. Cool before serving.

NOTE: How do I make oat flour?

One of the easiest healthy substitutions you can make in your baked recipes is to replace plain white flour with oat flour. Oat flour is essentially finely processed ground oats. Here's how to make it:

To replace 1 cup (125 g) of white flour, you will need 1 heaping cup (80 g) whole rolled oats, certified gluten-free if necessary. Pulse the oats in food processor/blender/coffee bean grinder until the oats resemble fine crumbs/flour.

OATMEAL CHOCOLATE CHIP COOKIES

CANCER FIGHTING - KID FRIENDLY - GLUTEN-FREE

Chocolate chip cookies are a great crowd-pleaser to share with friends and family. This cookie is reminiscent of the old-fashioned chocolate chip oatmeal cookies you may have grown up with.

MAKES 20 COOKIES

3 tbsp (45 ml) coconut oil, plus more for greasing pan

1½ cups (255 g) oat flour (see note)

1 cup (80 g) whole old-fashioned oats

½ tsp baking soda

½ tsp baking powder

1 tsp ground cinnamon

Pinch of sea salt

1 tsp natural vanilla extract

3 tbsp (34 g) natural almond butter

¼ cup (60 ml) maple syrup

½ cup (50 g) organic vegan dark chocolate (minimum 80 percent cacao), chopped into chunks

Preheat the oven to 350°F (177°C). Line a baking sheet with parchment paper and lightly brush it with coconut oil.

In a large bowl, combine the oat flour, whole oats, baking soda, baking powder, cinnamon and salt. Add the remaining ingredients, except the chocolate, and mix well. Once the coconut oil is well combined, add the chocolate.

Using clean hands, form 1-inch (25-mm) balls and place on baking sheet. Once you have finished using all the dough, use a fork and lightly press down on each cookie.

Bake for 10 minutes. Remove from the oven and let cool for at least 15 minutes. Do not overbake these cookies, especially if you prefer a chewier texture.

NOTE: **How do I make oat flour?**

One of the easiest healthy substitutions you can make in your baked recipes is to replace plain white flour with oat flour. Oat flour is essentially finely processed ground oats. Here is how to make it:

To replace 1 cup (125 g) of white flour, you will need 1 heaping cup (80 g) whole rolled oats, certified gluten-free if necessary. Pulse the oats in food processor/blender/coffee bean grinder until the oats resemble fine crumbs/flour.

DRESSINGS, SAUCES AND CONDIMENTS

Yes, condiments make everyday meals more exciting. Sure, it's easy to pick up a bottle of your favorite ketchup, dressing or barbecue sauce at the grocery store, but the challenge is that they are loaded with added sugar and highly processed oils, making them far from healthy! Many of the organic versions even contain ingredients that should be avoided. The good news is that making your own takes only a few minutes and you can control exactly what goes into it.

CREAMY RED PEPPER SAUCE

ANTI-INFLAMMATORY - CANCER FIGHTING - RICH IN VITAMIN C

This simple sauce is very versatile—it's great poured over roasted veggies, green salad, zoodles or as a dip. This combination is the perfect balance of savory, sweet and sour creamy goodness.

2 SERVINGS

3 organic red peppers, chopped

½ cup (20 g) fresh basil, chopped

½ cup (85 g) soaked almonds, drained (can substitute almond butter)

1 clove garlic

2 dates, pitted

3 tbsp (45 ml) apple cider vinegar

1 tbsp (10 g) nutritional yeast

1-inch (25-mm) piece of ginger, peeled

1 tsp dulse flakes

1 lemon, juiced

Place all of the ingredients in a high-speed blender or food processor. Blend until smooth. Pour over your favorite salad greens or zoodles or use as a veggie dip.

EASY VINAIGRETTE DRESSING

PROMOTES YOUTHFUL SKIN - DIGESTION - WEIGHT CONTROL

Eating our salads with dressing is not only tasty but is also a very good idea nutritionally. The right kind of fat is good for us, and most vitamins are fat soluble, which means that the vitamins in the salad veggies will be much better absorbed in the presence of a high-quality fat. This vinaigrette is a great way to ensure you get the most out of your salads.

2 SERVINGS

4 tbsp (60 ml) hemp oil

2 tbsp (30 ml) raw apple cider vinegar

2 tbsp (30 ml) maple syrup

1 lemon, juiced

¼ tsp sea salt

Place all of the ingredients in a mason jar, shake well and enjoy. Vinaigrette lasts in the refrigerator for 3 to 4 days.

MISO GINGER DRESSING

BENEFICIAL PROBIOTICS · ANTIVIRAL · IRON-RICH

There is a hippie vegetarian restaurant in Vancouver that makes an unbelievable miso ginger sauce. I knew from the first taste that I would need to come up with a recipe so I could have it whenever I wanted. This creation is quite possibly one of the most addictive dressings—its sweet and tangy flavors complement many dishes. You can serve it as a dipping sauce for wraps, use it as a salad dressing or drizzle it over steamed vegetables.

2 SERVINGS

1 cup (240 ml) water

¼ cup (45 g) raw tahini

1 tbsp (15 ml) maple syrup

2 tbsp (30 g) red or white unpasteurized miso

1-inch (25-mm) piece of ginger, peeled

1 tbsp (10 g) chia seeds, ground to a powder

1 tbsp (15 ml) raw apple cider vinegar

2 tsp (10 ml) fresh lime juice

Place all of the ingredients into a high-speed blender. Blend until silky smooth.

Set aside for 10 to 30 minutes, giving the chia seeds time to expand and absorb some of the dressing. Add more water if a thinner consistency is desired.

Store in the refrigerator for up to 5 days.

RAISIN CHUTNEY

EXCELLENT DIGESTIVE AID · REDUCES CONSTIPATION · BLOOD BUILDER

Chutneys are light, easy to make and rich in iron. They add a sweet, tangy and slightly spicy flavor to any dish. The chutney will keep for three weeks in the refrigerator and for up to six months in the freezer.

4 SERVINGS

1½ cups (227 g) raisins

½ apple, peeled and sliced

½ cup (120 ml) apple cider vinegar

Small piece of fresh ginger

1 clove garlic

Pinch of salt, optional

Cover the raisins in water and soak for 1 to 4 hours. Rinse and drain well.

Place all of the ingredients in a food processor or high-speed blender, and process until smooth.

Serve with Green Collard Wraps (page 138) or as a dip for veggies.

SUN-DRIED TOMATO BASIL MARINARA SAUCE

PROMOTES HEALTHY DIGESTION - ANTIVIRAL - HORMONAL SUPPORT

This sauce is easy, light and healthy. It's also very versatile. Use it as a dipping sauce for fresh veggies or crackers, on top of pizza or as a sauce for zoodles. The possibilities are endless!

2–3 SERVINGS

4 medium tomatoes, cut into quarters

¼ cup (38 g) chopped sun-dried tomatoes (not packed in oil)

1 clove garlic, peeled

⅓ cup (14 g) packed fresh basil leaves

½ cup (80 g) hemp seeds

½ lemon, juiced

¼ tsp Himalayan salt, optional

Put all of the ingredients in a blender and pulse until all are well-blended and the mixture is just slightly chunky.

HOMEMADE KETCHUP

EXCELLENT SOURCE OF VITAMIN C - IMMUNE BOOSTING - GREAT FOR SKIN AND HAIR

This is one of the easiest condiments to make. All you need are a few basic ingredients and a blender or food processor. If you like ketchup, it's a good idea to make a batch every few weeks to have it on hand to add to various dishes.

8 SERVINGS

¼ cup (38 g) sun-dried tomatoes

Small clove garlic

1-inch (25-mm) piece of ginger

1 tbsp (15 ml) balsamic vinegar

3 dates, pitted

1 cup (230 g) fresh cherry tomatoes

Blend all of the ingredients in a high-speed blender until creamy.

HERBALICIOUS PESTO

ANTI-INFLAMMATORY - BLOOD PURIFIER - HORMONE SUPPORT

Herbalicious Pesto is big on taste, without dairy. You won't miss the cheese, that's a promise. Pesto can be made from any combination of fresh herbs, nuts or seeds and good-quality oil. Be creative and find your own personal favorite combo.

2 SERVINGS

2½ heaping cups (100 g) fresh spinach

2 cups (80 g) fresh cilantro and parsley (feel free to try oregano, basil, thyme, etc.)

2–3 cloves garlic

½ cup (80 g) hemp seeds (can substitute with walnuts, pine nuts, cashews and sunflower seeds)

1 organic lemon, juiced and zested

2 tbsp (30 ml) flax oil or olive oil

3 tbsp (28 g) nutritional yeast

1 tsp white miso (optional)

Put the spinach, herbs, garlic, hemp seeds, lemon juice and zest in a food processor. Process until everything is combined and has a finely ground consistency.

Add the flax oil, nutritional yeast and miso and continue to process until you get a creamy sauce.

"THRIVE" CHEEZE SAUCE

GREAT SOURCE OF B_{12} - DAIRY-FREE - PROTEIN-RICH

"Thrive" Cheeze Sauce was inspired by one of my favorite lifestyle books, *Thrive* by Brendan Brazier. A few adjustments to the original created the best vegan cheese sauce I've ever made. It's thick and creamy and has a very cheese sauce–like texture. And the best part? The flavor!

MAKES 3 CUPS (720 ML)

1 cup (240 ml) filtered water

1 cup (150 g) nutritional yeast

½ cup (80 g) sunflower seeds (preferably soaked for 4 hours or overnight)

½ organic lemon, juiced and zested

1 clove garlic

1 tbsp (15 ml) coconut oil

½ tsp ground turmeric

¼ tsp sea salt

¼ tsp cayenne pepper

Place all of the ingredients in a high-speed blender and blend on high until smooth.

Transfer the sauce to a small saucepan and heat on low, stirring continuously for 3 to 5 minutes, or until the sauce thickens.

Remove from the heat and allow to sit for a couple of minutes before serving. This sauce is great for sandwiches, collard wraps, burritos or zoodles. Keep in the refrigerator for up to 1 week.

BLACK BEAN & PINEAPPLE SALSA

PREVENTS CANCER · IMPROVES DIGESTION · SUPPORTS WEIGHT LOSS

Don't know what to bring to a potluck? This homemade salsa—a mix of black beans and cilantro, tossed with sweet pineapple and tart lime juice—will have everyone talking.

3–4 SERVINGS

1 (15-oz [425-g]) can black beans, drained and rinsed (or 1½ cups [255 g] cooked)

¼ small pineapple, cored and chopped

1 handful cilantro, chopped

1 lime, juiced

1 tbsp (15 ml) apple cider vinegar

1 tsp ground cumin

¼ tsp cayenne pepper

Salt and pepper, to taste

In a large bowl, mix all of the ingredients together.

Makes a great appetizer, wrap or burrito filling, side salad or topping for black rice. Refrigerate up to 3 days.

HONEST SOUR CREAM

GREAT SOURCE OF CALCIUM · ANTI-INFLAMMATORY · HELPS WITH FAT LOSS

This simple vegan sour cream is wonderfully rich and tasty. Try it with chopped salads in place of mayonnaise, with any Mexican-inspired dishes or as a dip for vegetables or crackers.

4 SERVINGS

¼ cup (60 ml) full-fat coconut milk

½ cup (90 g) tahini

1 tbsp (15 ml) apple cider vinegar

Pinch of salt

Combine all of the ingredients in a blender and blend for 1 to 2 minutes until smooth. Store in the refrigerator in an airtight container for up to 5 days.

VEGAN PARMESAN

HIGH LEVELS OF B VITAMINS - GREAT SOURCE OF CALCIUM - DELICIOUS CHEESY FLAVOR

Nutritional yeast, with its slightly salty, nutty taste is what gives this recipe its cheese-like flavor. You can find nutritional yeast at most health food stores and can create this easy recipe in just a few minutes.

MAKES 2 CUPS (300 G)

1 cup (150 g) nutritional yeast flakes

1 cup (161 g) raw sesame seeds

1 tsp garlic powder

Mix all of the ingredients together in a high-speed blender or coffee grinder. Store cheese in the refrigerator to prevent it from going rancid. Use as a topping for zoodles, ratatouille, scrambled tempeh, sandwiches and more.

EASY GUACAMOLE

CARDIOVASCULAR SUPPORT - OSTEOPOROSIS PREVENTION - ANTI-INFLAMMATORY

Keep it original with this quick guacamole recipe. You can eat it with anything and everything, at all times of the day, it's that good.

4 SERVINGS

2 very ripe avocados

1 lime, juiced

½ cup (20 g) fresh cilantro, chopped

¼ medium white onion, minced

1 tsp salt

Chopped tomatoes, optional

Minced garlic, optional

Chili pepper flakes, optional

To cut the avocados, run a knife around the avocados (from top to bottom) and twist in half. Pull out and discard the pits. Using a spoon or your thumb, remove the flesh and place in a medium bowl.

Add the lime juice and mash the avocados with fork, leaving some chunks.

Gently stir in the cilantro, onion, salt and any/all of the optional ingredients.

Serve immediately.

THE BEST ORIGINAL HUMMUS

REGULATES BLOOD SUGAR - DIGESTIVE SUPPORT - BONE HEALTH

A basic chickpea hummus recipe is great to have on hand and is so versatile. It can be used as a dip for vegetables and served with crackers or sprouted bread; also use it as a spread for sandwiches and collard wraps.

3–4 SERVINGS

1½ cups (300 g) or 15-oz (425-g) can chickpeas

1 clove garlic, crushed

1 tsp sea salt

2 tbsp (30 ml) quality extra virgin olive oil or flax oil

3 tbsp (33 g) tahini

2 lemons, juiced

3 ice cubes

Organic lemon peel, optional

Paprika, optional

Cilantro or parsley leaves, optional

Rinse the chickpeas in cold water and add them to a food processor. Place all of the remaining ingredients in a food processor and blend until smooth. Store any remaining hummus in an airtight container in the refrigerator for up to 4 days.

PART 4

MY VEGAN KITCHEN

COOKING MADE SIMPLE

Both Nikki and I enjoy spending time in the kitchen. Cooking, baking and experimenting with healthy food is our passion. With that said, when it comes to day-to-day meal prep, we are all about efficiency. Our mission is to help you make healthy eating as simple as possible. The good news is you don't have to become a part-time chef.

If you are serious about your health and living plant-based, you will have to possess some basic cooking skills. The idea behind the majority of recipes you will find in this book is to teach you how to walk into your kitchen and whip up a tasty, plant-based meal from scratch in an average of 20 minutes.

In order for this to work, however, you'll need to have your kitchen well organized. A great kitchen setup can save you time, energy and stress.

HELPFUL KITCHEN TOOLS

ASSIGNMENT: FROM A TO Z

STEP #1

Throw away any pots, pans, skillets and baking sheets that have an aluminum surface or are Teflon coated. Nonstick cookware has been a real time saver in many kitchens, but there are some serious health concerns associated with aluminum and Teflon chemicals that can be released when heated. These chemicals can escape into our food and ultimately into our bodies. Many studies have linked exposure to these chemicals to a greater risk of thyroid disease, as well as having negative effects on your heart.

We also want you to seriously consider getting rid of as much plastic as possible, especially plastic food storage containers and water bottles. Replace them with glass, ceramic or stainless steel.

STEP #2

The following is a list of tools that will be quite helpful to have. You don't need to go out and buy everything on the list, but a few key pieces will make your cooking experience faster and more efficient.

Baking Pans and Cookie Sheets

Try to avoid any traditional bakeware such as nonstick and aluminum, as using them can cause hormone-disrupting chemicals and toxins to leach into food. Instead, choose ceramic, glass, cast iron or stoneware.

Basket Steamer

This handy kitchen gadget is an easy way to keep veggies healthy! Steaming vegetables will allow them to retain their color, texture and nutritional value.

Cast Iron Skillet

One of my secrets to consistent healthy eating is using cast iron. It's perfect for one-dish meals, it makes your vegetables taste amazing and even adds a trace amount of beneficial iron to your food. It's also durable, lasts forever and is up for just about any task you need.

Food Processor

Another helpful tool, you will use a food processor for chopping veggies, making bean dips, sauces, raw burgers, cookie and cake batters—you name it. We can't imagine our kitchens without them, as they save us a bunch of preparation time.

Food Storage Containers

Storage containers are a must! Get a glass set with different sizes. Small containers are great for dressings, dips and sauces, while larger ones will come in handy for your work or school lunches, saving leftovers and having pre-chopped veggies ready for salads and dinner meals.

Garlic Press

So you peeled the garlic cloves. Now what? If you are like us and dread mincing garlic, get a garlic press. You will be happy that you did, it's quick and your hands will be spared of the lingering garlic odor.

High-Quality Water Filter

Avoid drinking and cooking with tap water without filtering it first. Either buy water from your health food store, get your water delivered to your home, find a natural spring or buy a high-quality filter and filter your tap water yourself. This will save you from ingesting heavy metals, chlorine, pesticides and other contaminants.

Juicer

We are big proponents of drinking fresh homemade juices daily. When you juice raw vegetables, you gain almost all of their natural nutrients, including antioxidant phytochemicals. You can easily include an extra 5 to 10 servings of fruit and vegetables in one large glass of fresh green juice. Those nutrients offer enormous health benefits, including weight loss and reduction in chronic disease. You can find a juicer for any budget, ranging from $30 to thousands of dollars.

Manual Citrus Juicer

This tool saves us a lot of time in the kitchen. Is it essential to have one? No, however, the citrus press/juicer is a handy tool when you are in a hurry. Not to mention it saves you the frustration of dealing with the unwanted seeds.

Mason Jars

Mason jars are sturdy, come in a wide variety of shapes and sizes, can often be found inexpensively and best of all, they are a completely nontoxic way to store things in your kitchen! From smoothies, juices, homemade nut butters and leftovers to packing up your weekday lunches, you will always find a use for them.

Mortar and Pestle

This old-school kitchen tool is awesome for grinding fresh herbs and spices. We also use it to make homemade hummus, pesto and guacamole. Can you use an electric grinder? Sure, but the flavors and texture are just not the same.

Nut Milk Bag

If you plan on making your own nut and seed milks, you will need one of these. They are super cheap and can double up as a simple fruit and vegetable juicer.

Slow Cooker

Using a slow cooker is a great way to save time and still prepare a nutritious meal. Assemble the meal in the morning, put it in the slow cooker and at the end of the day, dinner is ready—without much mess or many dishes to clean.

Spiralizer

We love this tool! It's essential for making low-carb, gluten-free noodles from zucchini, sweet potato, carrots, cucumbers and almost any other veggie. You can use veggie noodles as pasta or as a base for wraps and salads.

Sprouting Jar

Sprout your own nuts, grains and seeds in less than a week. You can also make your own by covering a large mason jar with cheesecloth or a nylon stocking and securing with a rubber band or string. We have a do-it-yourself version on our site.

Vitamix or Other High-Speed Blender

We suggest you look into getting a high-speed blender such as a Vitamix. The initial investment is a bit higher, but it's worth every penny. You will be using it to blend smoothies, soups, dressings, sauces, yogurts, Nicecreams and many other daily essentials. We use our Vitamix multiple times a day and sometimes even travel with it.

Zester

We like the Microplane zester. They're ideal for lemons and limes, but also work well for finely grating nutmeg, ginger and garlic.

KITCHEN SETUP RESOURCES AVAILABLE FOR YOU AT WWW.ACTIVEVEGETARIAN.COM

We Can't Live Without . . . Our Top Favorite Kitchen Tools, Reviewed (article)

SOAKING AND SPROUTING

Perhaps you have noticed that some of our recipes call for soaked or sprouted nuts, seeds, beans or grains. In this chapter you will learn some of the basics behind soaking and sprouting and the benefits that go along with them.

WHY SOAK AND SPROUT?

Nuts, seeds, beans, legumes and certain grains are an essential part of a healthy vegan diet. They are often considered power foods and heavily utilized in many vegan recipes. Unfortunately, a large number of people avoid them and miss out on their tremendous health benefits. The common complaint is indigestion, bloating and gas associated with eating foods like beans or nuts.

There is a reason for this issue. And there is also a solution. So let's look at it closer to help you understand.

When you purchase raw seeds (nuts, grains and legumes included), they are in their dormant state, waiting for their opportunity to grow. Inside of the seed is everything needed to create life—enzymes, proteins, minerals and healthy fats. However, these nutrients are not active; they are locked inside the seed, protected and waiting for the right time to start expressing their potential.

This protection is created by a naturally occurring chemical called phytic acid. Whenever we ingest unsoaked, unsprouted seeds or food made out of them, this acid will cause troubles in our digestive tract. It inhibits our digestive system's ability to break this food down properly and can cause indigestion, gas and bloating.

Phytic acid also binds to minerals like zinc, iron, magnesium, calcium, chromium and manganese in our gut. Eating too many poorly prepared seeds, nuts, legumes and grains could lead to mineral deficiency (such as anemia) and also contribute to poor bone density. Eating nuts, seeds and legumes is super beneficial to a vegan diet, but it's important to get the full nutritional potential of these foods. For that reason, we suggest always soaking and/or sprouting prior to eating or cooking with them.

SOAKING

Nature is incredibly smart. Let's take a sunflower seed, for example. If the seed is stored dry in your pantry, it won't just start sprouting and growing. However, if the same seed is provided with water and light for a sufficient amount of time, it will start to come alive. The water will release the phytic acid and allow enzymes to be wakened, as well as to supply itself with abundant energy. For us it simply means an increase in vitamins, especially B vitamins, as well as easier digestion and absorption of nutrients.

WHAT DO YOU NEED TO START SOAKING?

Place a seed of choice in a large glass bowl or mason jar and cover with warm, filtered water (about a 2:1 ratio) and about ½ teaspoon Celtic sea salt. Cover with a light cloth.

Leave in a warm place for a specified time—refer to the Sprouting chart on page 185. Rinse seeds thoroughly, drain and use.

SPROUTING

Sprouting takes this seed business into a whole new level. By completing several cycles of soaking, rinsing, draining and air exposure, certain seeds will enter a state of germination and actually grow little tails. This is super beneficial for us as it multiplies the content of minerals and vitamins in the seed many times. Vitamins A, B complex, C and E are increased—sometimes as much as ten times![1]

---

1   Márton, M., Z. Mándoki, Z. Csapó-Kiss and J. Csapó, "The role of sprouts in human nutrition. A review," Sapientia University. http://www.acta.sapientia.ro/acta-alim/C3/alim3-5.pdf.

SOAKING& SPROUTING times

💧 SOAKING TIMES	🌱 SPROUTING TIMES

NUTS & SEEDS

	Soaking	Sprouting		Soaking	Sprouting
ALL (avoid peanuts) 1 cup (161 g)= 1¾ cups (282 g)	12 hours	N/A	**PUMPKIN** (hulled) 1 cup (161 g)= 1¾ cups (282 g) (soak in cool water, store dry in fridge)	4 hours	12–24 hours
ALMONDS 1 cup (170 g)= 1¾ cups (300 g)	12 hours	1-2 days	**SESAME** (hulled) 1 cup (161 g)= 1½ cups (240 g) (soak in cool water, do not sprout longer or they'll be bitter)	4 hours	6–12 hours
SUNFLOWER (hulled) 1 cup (125 g)= 2 cups (250 g) (soak in cool water, store dry in fridge)	4 hours	12-24 hours	**BUCKWHEAT** (hulled) 1 cup (170 g)= 1¾ cups (300 g) (soak in cool water, do not sprout longer or they'll be bitter)	1-4 hours	12–24 hours

BEANS & LEGUMES

	Soaking	Sprouting		Soaking	Sprouting
LENTILS ½ cup (100 g)= 2 cups (400 g) (soak in very warm water to convert starches to complex sugars)	12 hours	3 days	**MUNG** ½ cup (100 g)= 4 cups (800 g) (soak in very warm water initially)	12 hours	3 days
CHICKPEAS (garbanzos) ½ cup (100 g)= 2 cups (400 g) (soak in very warm water initially, complete protein)	12 hours	3 days	**LIMA/PINTO/WHITE/RED** ½ cup (100 g)= 2 cups (400 g) (soak in very warm water initially)	12 hours	3 days
ADZUKI ½ cup (100 g)= 4 cups (800 g) (soak in very warm water initially)	12 hours	4 days	**GREEN PEAS** ½ cup (75 g)= 1½ cups (227 g) (soak in very warm water initially)	12 hours	3 days

GRAINS

	Soaking	Sprouting		Soaking	Sprouting
WHEAT/KAMUT 1 cup (125 g)= 3 cups (375 g) (soak in very warm water initially)	6 hours	2 days	**BARLEY** 1 cup (185 g)= 2½ cups (460 g) (soak in very warm water initially)	6 hours	3 days
SPELT 1 cup (125 g)= 3 cups (375 g) (soak in very warm water initially)	6 hours	2 days	**CORN** ½ cup (72 g)= 2 cups (288 g) (soak in very warm water initially)	12 hours	2 days
RYE 1 cup (125 g)= 3 cups (375 g) (soak in very warm water initially)	6 hours	2 days			

ALKALIZING GRAINS

	Soaking	Sprouting		Soaking	Sprouting
QUINOA 1 cup (125 g)= 3 cups (375 g) (soak in very warm water initially, most calcium)	3–6 hours	24 hours	**AMARANTH** 1 cup (125 g)= 3 cups (375 g) (soak in very warm water initially)	3–6 hours	24 hours
MILLET 1 cup (125 g)= 3 cups (375 g) (soak in very warm water initially, most alkalizing of grains)	6 hours	12 hours	**TEFF** 1 cup (125 g) = 3 cups (375 g) (soak in very warm water initially)	3–6 hours	24 hours

Both the quantity and quality of the protein in most sprouts are dramatically increased. Due to new amino acids found in sprouts, we are able to better digest the food. Sprouts are full of new vibrancy and including them into your diet will transfer their life energy to your body.

All flours used can be made from sprouted and/or fermented grains for easier digestion. Unfortunately, this is no longer a common procedure and is often the reason behind so many grain/gluten allergies. Our recommendation is to eat as many of your grains sprouted as possible. There are several companies on the market that are going back to sprouted grains. Our favorite is Ezekiel 4:9 by Food For Life. You can find their products in the frozen section of your local health food store.

THE MANY BENEFITS OF SPROUTING

Alkalizing

Our blood must maintain a delicate pH balance of 7.365. We need a balance of acid to alkaline food to maintain good health. Unfortunately, we usually have too many acid-forming foods in our diet (stress and environmental stresses can lower our pH, making our body more acidic). On the other hand, the chlorophyll in sprouts helps offset this acidity by oxygenating our cells.[2]

Bio-Available Nutrition

As sprouts grow, their nutrients increase greatly and are easily assimilated by the body.

Easy

Sprouting is as easy as placing viable seeds in contact with pure water!

Highly Digestible

Sprouting reduces the enzyme inhibitors that keep the seed or grain dormant until it is ready to grow. Reducing the inhibitors activates the enzymes, resulting in pre-digested, easy-to-absorb nutrition.[29]

---

2   Chung, TY, EN Nwokolo, JS Sim, "Compositional and digestibility changes in sprouted barley and canola seeds," Plant Foods for Human Nutrition 39 (1989): 267-78.

Quality Protein

Germination causes the seeds to become pre-digested amino acids and simple sugars. Unlike cooked proteins, the amino acids of raw sprouts don't coagulate, making them easier for the body to absorb.[3]

Fresh

Sprouts can be prepared year-round and are full of energy.

Variety

There are many varieties of seeds, beans and grains that can be sprouted for different flavors, textures and nutrition.

Cheap

It costs pennies to produce pounds of greens.

Low in Calories

Sprouts are a wonderful food for anyone watching their weight. Considering their high nutritional value, they are relatively low in calories.

WHAT DO YOU NEED TO START SPROUTING?

For an instructional video on how to soak and sprout seeds go to www.activevegetarian.com.

There is no fancy equipment required. You will need:

- A jar (ideally a sprouting jar from your local health food store) or a mason jar
- Filtered water
- Muslin cloth/cheesecloth
- Elastic band or ribbon (not needed if you have a jar with a two-part lid)
- Sprouting nut/bean/seed of choice

HOW LONG WILL MY SPROUTS TAKE TO GROW?

The great news is that after only a few days, most sprouts will be ready to eat. The longer the sprout time, the larger their tails will grow and the more sprout-y they will become. Different nuts and seeds take longer to germinate, so refer to the Soaking & Sprouting Times Chart on page 185 to get an idea of how long each sprout will take to be ready.

---

3   Chavan, JK, SS Kadam, "Nutritional improvement of cereals by sprouting," Critical Reviews in Food Science and Nutrition 28 (1989):401-37.

Be aware that the smaller the sprout, the more prone it will be to mold. It's important to be consistent with rinsing and make sure to drain them well every time you give them a rinse.

FOUR SIMPLE STEPS TO SPROUTING:

Step 1

Soak the seeds, nuts, grains or legumes as per the sprouting chart (page 185).

Step 2

Rinse with fresh filtered water twice daily.

Step 3

Store upside down in a glass jar with cheesecloth over the top or in a sprouting bag. Don't allow sprouts to sit in water.

Step 4

Expose the sprouts to sunlight to increase chlorophyll (the blood of plants).

WAYS TO EAT SPROUTS:

- As a snack
- In a stir-fry
- On top of soup
- Mixed in salads
- Layered on sandwiches
- Inside tortillas
- With breakfast cereals

SOAKING AND SPROUTING RESOURCES AVAILABLE FOR YOU AT WWW.ACTIVEVEGETARIAN.COM:

- How to Soak and Sprout Seeds (video)
- DIY Sprouting Jar (video and infographic)

SHOULD YOU BUY ORGANIC?

You might be holding an organic apple in one hand and a conventional one in the other, wondering, "Why the heck should I buy organic? They both look the same and the conventional apple is cheaper, so why can't I just buy that?" Visually they may look alike, but there are some major differences.

How your food is grown can have a significant impact on your mental and emotional health, as well as the environment. Organic foods often have more beneficial nutrients, such as antioxidants, than their conventionally grown counterparts. Many people with allergies to foods, chemicals or preservatives often find their symptoms lessen or go away when they switch to organic foods.

Conventionally grown grains, fruits and vegetables are known to contain all sorts of chemicals, pesticides and growth hormones, and often are genetically modified. Chemicals like these found in everyday foods disrupt the function of our hormones and may cause many serious health issues from heart disease, diabetes and high cholesterol to weight gain and obesity. [4]

In the best-case scenario, we would buy all our produce organic to ensure our food is as clean as possible, but that can be quite unrealistic.

The first challenge is the price. Organic produce tends to be more expensive than conventionally grown produce, and our budgets might not always allow for that.

The second challenge is availability. Not all grocery stores carry our favorite produce with the organic label.

Here are three simple tips that we personally find very helpful:

EAT LOCAL AND WHAT'S IN SEASON

If you can go to a local market or produce stand—this is a great option. Eating what is in season limits imported produce consumption and means what you're eating hasn't been sprayed to extend its life-span. Ask questions about the produce—who's the grower and where did it come from?

---

4   The Environmental Working Group. "Research," last modified 2017, http://www.ewg.org/research#.WXCuGv_ytBw.

GROW YOUR OWN

If you can be self-sufficient, this is a great way to consume fruits and veggies. You know exactly how they were grown and most of what is in the surrounding soil. And to be honest, wouldn't it just taste better knowing that you grew it? Talk about a connection with your food and the time and love you gave it.

FOLLOW THE DIRTY DOZEN/CLEAN FIFTEEN RULE

The Environmental Working Group (EWG) puts all of our favorite fruits and vegetables under a series of careful tests and every year releases a list called the Dirty Dozen and Clean Fifteen. This list is a great tool to help us make smarter choices and guide us consumers in the right direction when selecting our produce. Making informed choices in the produce aisle helps minimize pesticide consumption while keeping the cost down.

Whenever possible, buy organic when purchasing the produce listed under the Dirty Dozen, or avoid it altogether.

On the other hand, items listed under the Clean Fifteen are relatively safe to buy non-organic. This means that only a few pesticides were detected on these foods and tests found low total concentrations of pesticides on them.

HOW DO I KNOW IT'S ORGANIC?

The PLU (or Price Look Up) code on produce stickers indicates a number of factors and can be helpful to consumers in a few ways. Primarily, it is an easy way to identify conventional versus organic produce at the market.

Four Numbers = Non-Organic

If there are only four numbers in the PLU, this means that the produce was grown conventionally with the use of pesticides.

Eight = GMO

If there are five numbers in the PLU code and the number starts with "8," then this tells you that the item is a genetically modified fruit or vegetable. Genetically modified foods are NEVER organic!

Nine = Organic

If there are five numbers in the PLU code and the number starts with "9," this is a sign to tell you that the produce has been grown organically and is not genetically modified.

TIP: Leafy greens and hot peppers were frequently found to be contaminated with a toxin that can be very harmful to the human nervous system. Grow your own or buy organic always!

SHOULD YOU BUY ORGANIC RESOURCES AVAILABLE FOR YOU AT WWW.ACTIVEVEGETARIAN.COM

- Dirty Dozen and Clean Fifteen (video)

ACKNOWLEDGMENTS

THANK YOU.

Special thanks to our amazing clients, many of whom we now consider family, especially Denise, Gazal, Geoff and Lisa, Hannah, Ingrid, Khangmin, Mary, Michelle, Morgan, Nina, Paul, Sergey, Shannon and Sharon. Without your support, love and encouragement, this book would not exist. So much of who we are is because of what we have learned from you. For that we will always be thankful.

To Zoe and Marco. Thank you for your kindness and support.

To our loving families for allowing us the freedom to go our own way and for supporting our dreams no matter how crazy they might have seemed.

To our friend John. Thank you for housing such a generous and beautiful soul.

To our friend Missy, for always believing in us and reminding us to follow our heart.

To our teacher, Acharya Vinay, for guiding us toward light.

Our wonderful photographer, Darina, for capturing the beauty of plant-based foods.

To Page Street Publishing, for your belief in this book and your faith in us. Thanks as well to Elizabeth and the rest of the team for investing your energy in this project.

And last but not least, to our fans and followers all over the world for continuously challenging us to be our best.

With love and gratitude for you all!

—Zuzana and Nikki

ABOUT THE AUTHORS

Zuzana Fajkusova and Nikki Lefler are fitness coaches, lifestyle mentors and creators of the blog Active Vegetarian, a plant-based eater's guide to fitness, nutrition and lifestyle.

Together, they are on a mission to engage and inspire as many people as possible to live healthier, more active and more sustainable lives.

The *Vegan Weight Loss Manifesto* is their way to share personal knowledge and offer a practical guide in this fast-paced world.

INDEX